making and flying
MODERN KITES

making and flying MODERN KITES

Jim Rowlands

illustrated by
JOHN CROOKS

Dryad Press Ltd London

ACKNOWLEDGEMENT

During the year that this book took to research and write I have of course received lots of help, support and encouragement from a number of friends and colleagues which I should like to acknowledge. Thanks to John Crooks for the illustrations; Bill Souten, John Spendlove and Fred Waterhouse for the loan of their kite libraries; Dan Leigh, Martin Lester, Mark Cottrell, Jon and Gill Bloom and Paul Chapman for their help and advice; Helen Bushell, Ed Grauel, Peter Lynn, David Pelham, Martin Powell, Jacques Zanni, Ken Sams, Tony Cartwright, Francis Rogallo, Steven Sutton and Margaret Greger for allowing their designs to be reproduced.

And final thanks of course must go to my wife Ann, who despite undergoing some painful surgery during the past year was still able to offer her support, advice and encouragement.

Jim Rowlands
June 1987

ISBN 0 8521 9741 1

Typeset by Servis Filmsetting Ltd, Manchester
and printed in Great Britain by
The Bath Press Ltd
Bath.
for the publishers
Dryad Press Ltd
8 Cavendish Square
London W1M OAJ

contents

preface

I was four years old when I made and flew my first kite. It was a design of my father's and strange even by today's standards, a sort of Rogallo Flexikite, made from brown wrapping paper, but with the wings brought forward to create two tubes. As I remember it didn't fly too well and needed a long crepe paper tail to keep it stable. But this simple paper kite entertained me throughout the summer months which from my father's point of view, I suppose, was more important than its aerodynamics.

Thirty years later I returned to kiteflying, much to the bewilderment of my wife and family. Designs had changed, materials had changed, yet – nothing had changed. The joy, the fun, the peace, the tranquillity, the excitement, the magic that this seemingly pointless pastime brings were all still there. And I was hooked yet again.

For several years now I have been spending my summers presenting kitemaking workshops and *Making and Flying Modern Kites* was written in response to many requests to supply details of designs, sources of materials and techniques used. I have tried to respond to all of these requests and include something for everyone: schoolteacher, youth leader, playgroup worker, novice kiteflier as well as for the ardent enthusiast.

But concentrating on 'modern' kites, those made popular during the past forty years, does not dismiss the previous four thousand as unimportant. On the contrary, eastern influences are still very strong. And despite the rapid developments in design and greater understanding of aerodynamics, kites are once again becoming appreciated not just as children's toys but as an art form, worthy of serious study. An approach solidly based on eastern teachings.

Most of the designs featured in later chapters are either classic modern designs, or those I have featured in workshops, with one or two of my personal favourites. As well as suggesting construction materials each kite is graded according to difficulty. Those graded * can be tackled by younger children and are suitable for group workshops, whereas the fabric kites graded **** should only be attempted by experienced kitemakers. All of them have been made and tested and will fly in the wind conditions indicated.

CHAPTER ONE

introduction

As an exercise at the start of one of my workshops, I asked the participants to draw a picture of a kite without copying or conferring with a neighbour. Almost without exception they returned sketches of either flat, diamond shapes with two cross-spars to the corners or square box kites – archetypal 'kite'-shaped kites, as one later described them.

What I try to do in workshops, and what I hope to do here, is to introduce some of the developments in kite design and construction which have taken place over the past forty years. During this time kitemakers have been less concerned with the aerodynamics of flight, the obsession of their predecessors, and have given more attention to colour, pattern, shape and form, bringing a totally different approach to their craft. Both kitemakers and kitefliers are also slowly beginning to recognise some of the eastern teachings, appreciating kites not just as efficient lifting devices or the play-things of children, but as aerial sculptures, artistic performances, to be admired as much for their beauty, elegance and craftsmanship as for their flying characteristics.

As part of this revival, a whole new range of materials has come within reach of the kitemaker. Rip-stop nylon, fibreglass and injection moulded plastics have each allowed designers to experiment in a different way with new shapes and configurations. Box kites with multiple wings; stickless kites which fly in the lightest of breezes; spinning kites whose flight defies explanation and the giant parafoils, so light yet so powerful. All are products of this modern era of kite design.

Why people fly kites still remains a mystery. After all, standing in the middle of a field holding on to a piece of string must be one of the more pointless ways of spending a Sunday afternoon. But the only people who don't understand why others fly kites are perhaps those who have never tried.

Some writers talk of the Zen of kiting, a fusion of the mind and the elements, inducing an inner peace, to leave you renewed and refreshed. Others try to explain it in more concrete terms, that kiteflying provides both relaxation and exercise at the same time. But the answer may be much simpler than this – people fly kites because they enjoy doing

so. And most of us don't need any reason other than that!

There is, as I take pains to point out in my workshops, much more to kite design than flat diamonds and square boxes. And the variety of modern kite shapes is something which newcomers often find bewildering.

Despite this seemingly wide diversity, however, kites can be grouped into seven categories, according to the type of construction illustrated in Fig 1.1 (a)–(g).

Plane surface kites (Fig 1.1 (a)) are those made of single or multiple sails stretched across a frame and can either be flat or bowed, flown with a keel or multiple bridles, tailed or tailless.

Box kites (Fig 1.1 (b)) are three-dimensional designs, again made up of a pattern of sails stretched across a framework, creating both lifting and stabilising surfaces.

The delta (Fig 1.1 (c)) is a special form of plane surface kite. Generally triangular, the spars are fitted so that the flexible sail forms two conical sections about a central keel.

The sled (Fig 1.1 (d)) is another flexible kite whose unique feature is the lack of horizontal spars.

All the previous configurations consist of flat sails in combination. Parafoils on the other hand are made up of enclosed aerofoil sections which inflate in the wind. (Fig 1.1 (e).)

Windsock or inflatable kites (Fig 1.1 (f)) are perhaps not pure kites, since they do not generate any lifting force, but when the concept is used to create a hybrid, say with a parafoil or flat kite, for example, they open up the boundaries of design – which to judge by recent innovations are limitless.

Rotor kites are different again and depend for their flight characteristics on a phenomena called the 'Magnus' effect. Here the lifting force is created by the spinning action of the kite. (Fig 1.1 (g).)

Like most other specialist hobbies kiteflying has its share of jargon and buzz words. To the layman they are perhaps just meaningless gibberish, but to understand much of kite design and construction, not only in later chapters but also in the company of other kitefliers, a short course in 'Kitespeak' is almost obligatory. Several standard terms describing the kite are illustrated in Fig 1.2.

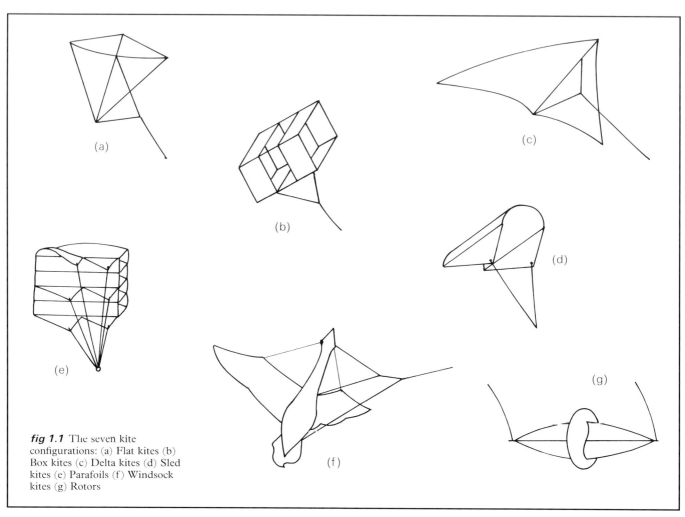

fig 1.1 The seven kite configurations: (a) Flat kites (b) Box kites (c) Delta kites (d) Sled kites (e) Parafoils (f) Windsock kites (g) Rotors

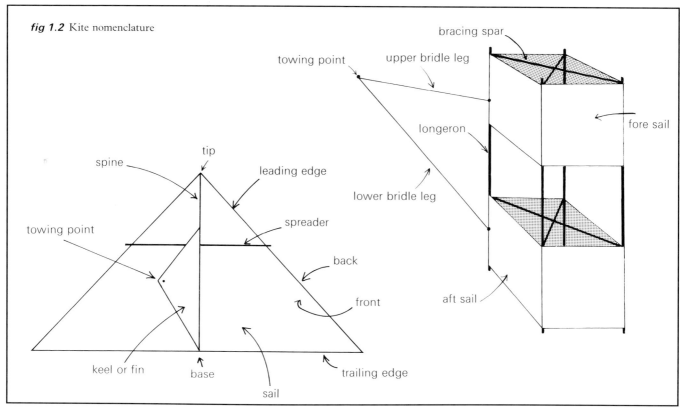

fig 1.2 Kite nomenclature

towing point

upper bridle leg

bracing spar

fore sail

longeron

lower bridle leg

aft sail

spine

tip

leading edge

spreader

back

front

towing point

keel or fin

base

sail

trailing edge

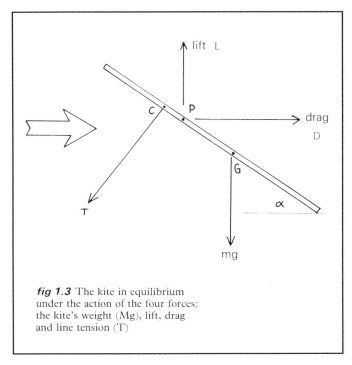

fig 1.3 The kite in equilibrium
under the action of the four forces:
the kite's weight (Mg), lift, drag
and line tension (T)

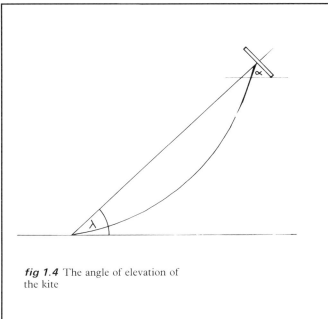

fig 1.4 The angle of elevation of
the kite

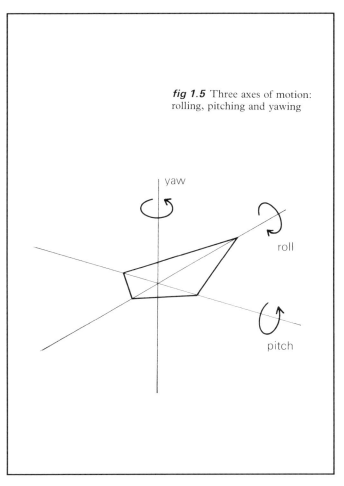

fig 1.5 Three axes of motion:
rolling, pitching and yawing

All four forces are balanced with the plane of the kite inclined at an angle α to the direction of the wind, referred to as the angle of attack.

The values of lift and drag vary with the angle of attack and wind speed and for a given wind speed there is one angle when the lift is maximum, described as the stalling angle. The position of the towing point C is usually set so that the kite flies just below the stalling angle. In an increasing gust therefore the kite will normally rise, as the lifting force increases, rather than fall, the consequence of increased drag.

The angle of elevation, λ is the angle of the kite relative to the anchor point – the flier (Fig 1.4). Although technically incorrect, 'aspect-ratio' is usually understood to mean the ratio of the width of the kite to its length.

The kite, as well as rising and falling with changing wind speeds, can also move about three axes which for the sake of convenience we shall assume intersect at some point on the kite (Fig. 1.5). Motion about the vertical axis (base – tip) is referred to as rolling; motion about the horizontal axis is called pitching; and motion about an axis perpendicular to both of these is called yawing.

A very narrow yaw in a kite is quite acceptable, almost beneficial as it turns with the changing air currents. Similarly with pitching, particularly on flat kites and deltas. But one which continually wanders across the sky, rolling back and forth, is not so much inefficient as a hazard. And to fly such a kite is both dangerous and reckless.

Even if I fully understood the subject myself, an explanation of kite aerodynamics would occupy the rest of the book and require some complex mathematics, much of it irrelevant to practical day-to-day kiteflying and making. But again there are some basic concepts which need to be understood.

When a kite is flying stably in the wind it is subject to four forces as indicated in Fig 1.3; the line tension T, its weight Mg and two forces created by the interaction of the wind against the sail – a force parallel to the wind direction described as drag – D, and a force perpendicular to the wind direction called lift – L. These latter two forces are considered to be acting at a point P, called the centre of pressure.

CHAPTER TWO

evolution of modern kites

PLANE-SURFACE KITES

From their origins in China over four thousand years ago plane-surface kites, flown either flat or bowed, have found their way to almost all regions of the world; eastwards through Japan and Korea; south through Indo-China and the Malay Peninsula to Indonesia and Australasia; and westward via the trade routes to Thailand, Burma, India, the Middle East and North Africa, eventually arriving in Europe during the fourteenth century.

Plane-surface kites all share a simple structure, consisting of a sail, usually of a regular geometric shape, stretched across a wooden/twine framework. But within the basic pattern there is, of course, a multitude of variations. As designs were passed from one region to the next, they were adapted to accommodate local materials to create the diversity of shapes and patterns we have today.

In his book *Kites: an Historical Survey* Clive Hart charts the development of two distinct kite types in Europe. The first he describes as 'dragon' or 'pennon' kites which had flat, square sails, usually painted with the image of a dragon, with multiple cross-spars to the front. In form they resembled many eastern kites and were used in battle for much the same purposes, but, according to Hart, were developed independently.

By the seventeenth century pennon kites had gone out of fashion and in their place had come figure and diamond kites, brought to Europe by sailors travelling the eastern trade routes. In contrast to the pennons these kites were light, graceful and very easy to fly. And it was during this period that the practice of kiteflying changed from the serious sport of adults to the play of children; an image which twentieth-century adult kitefliers are still trying to overcome.

The two most popular shapes of the eighteenth and nineteenth centuries were the 'Lozenge' (symmetrical diamond) and the 'Pear Top', both of which were flown with long tails. The Pear Top is usually regarded as the only indigenous European kite, but few are seen on the kite-fields of today. The diamond, on the other hand, has remained very popular, although twentieth-century versions differ considerably from those enjoyed by Victorian fliers.

Despite these ancient origins, modern designs abound. Alick Pearson's 'Roller', with its split sail, possesses considerably improved lifting qualities. A well-constructed Roller, for example, will sit quite comfortably at 500 metres in the lightest of winds – hauling it down is usually the difficult part. David Pelham's 'Flare' and 'Multi-flare' are two more unique modern creations.

The derivation of Richard Hewitt's 'Flexkite' is not quite so clear. Unkind critics describe it as the Hewitt 'Floppy' kite which, given the chance, will bite a chunk out of everything else in the sky. But the Flexkite is not without character, and is infinitely variable. Helen Bushell's menagerie of birds and fish, for example, is entirely based on Richard's original design (Fig 2.1).

A sub-group of this family is what might be called jib-rigged sail kites. The sail groupings on these designs resemble those on sailing boats and some configurations, such as 'Clipper' and 'Schooner', bear their names. The 'Marconi' rig, for example, was first introduced on a winged box kite in 1948 by Mack Angus and has since evolved into a plane-surface kite (Fig 2.2). Most jib-rigged kites, however, are very individual to their makers and few have been manufactured commercially.

Plane-surface kites are currently undergoing a revival, principally through the interest of artists seeing kites as a novel, creative medium. Kite painting, established with the first kites of China, is slowly gaining recognition here in the West. And whereas we once regarded a kitemaker's skill as the ability to produce a light, stable and efficient kite, our values are changing as we also consider aspects such as colour, pattern, shape and form.

Artists such as Canada's Skye Morrison; Australia's Leon Pericles, Helen Bushell and Peter Travis; America's Tal Streeter, Jacqueline Monnier and Tom Van Sant, and Britain's Martin Lester, Steve Brockett and Gill Bloom all have worldwide reputations, not for their engineering skills, but for their imagination, creativity and originality in transforming the kite into a work of art, the science into the aesthetic. Flying is almost secondary.

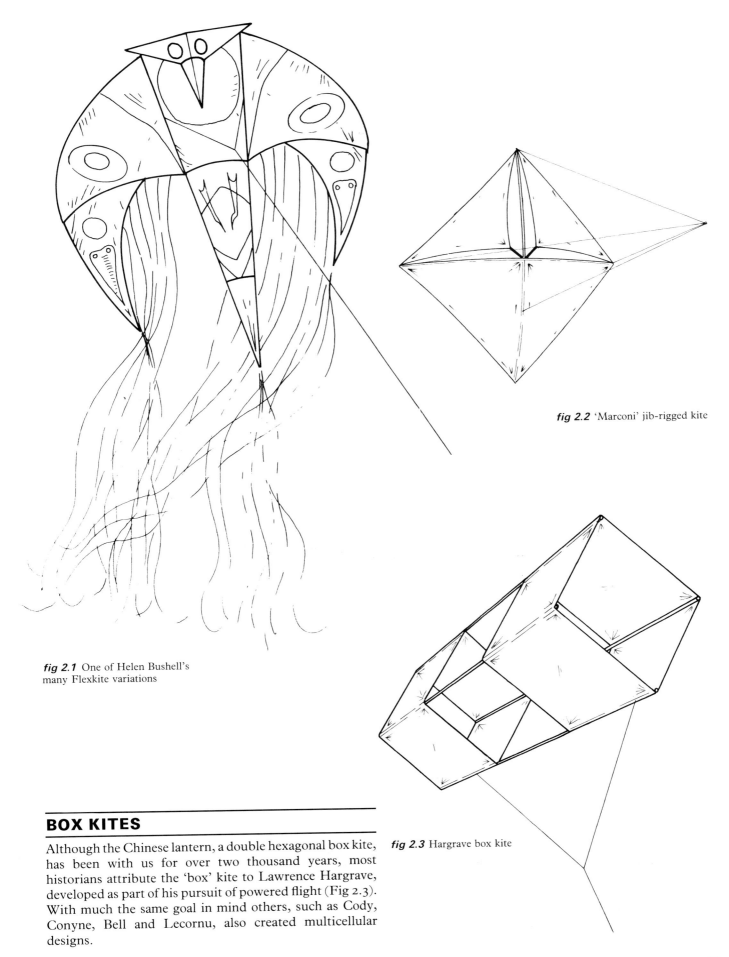

fig 2.1 One of Helen Bushell's many Flexkite variations

fig 2.2 'Marconi' jib-rigged kite

fig 2.3 Hargrave box kite

BOX KITES

Although the Chinese lantern, a double hexagonal box kite, has been with us for over two thousand years, most historians attribute the 'box' kite to Lawrence Hargrave, developed as part of his pursuit of powered flight (Fig 2.3). With much the same goal in mind others, such as Cody, Conyne, Bell and Lecornu, also created multicellular designs.

In 1910 Paul Flaix published details of a kite made up of two square sails joined along a diagonal, thus creating four wings set at right angles (Fig 2.4). At the time both Mr Flaix and his kite were largely ignored, but this one design, perhaps more than any other, has influenced the evolution of the modern box.

In a move away from the traditional configuration, Francis Rogallo used the form of the Flaix to produce his 'Corner Kite', in which two externally-braced cells share a single spine. As with his Flexikite, this kite was developed with a more serious application in mind, as a radar reflector. But with recent interest in externally-braced kites, it has been enjoying renewed popularity among home constructors.

The single Rogallo cell was clearly the main influence for Stephen Robinson's 'Facet' (Fig 2.5). Here the sail can be square or diamond-shaped, but the main feature of the design is its additional sails, subdividing the cells to create a snowflake pattern. While Stephen is rarely seen flying anything but four-sided versions, albeit in multiples, the facet can be built with three, four, five, six (or more?) sides, of high or low aspect-ratio, large or small. It is, without doubt, one of the most interesting contributions to modern box kite design.

Another remarkable box kite comes from New Zealand's Peter Lynn. In some respects it is similar to the Rogallo Corner Kite, but each 'cell' is made up of three, rather than four, wings and the structure internally braced (Fig 2.6). This rather unique sail configuration has imparted substantial lift and stability to the design, giving it the 'feel' of a delta rather than a standard box, and the *PLT* has surprised many a novice flier.

In the ten years since its introduction Peter Waldron's 'Prof Waldof Box' (Fig 2.7) has become one of those classic designs which has been copied, adapted and copied again. Essentially a multi-cell winged, hexagon box, its clever geometry combines with Peter's high manufacturing standards to produce a light, efficient, stable and very popular kite indeed.

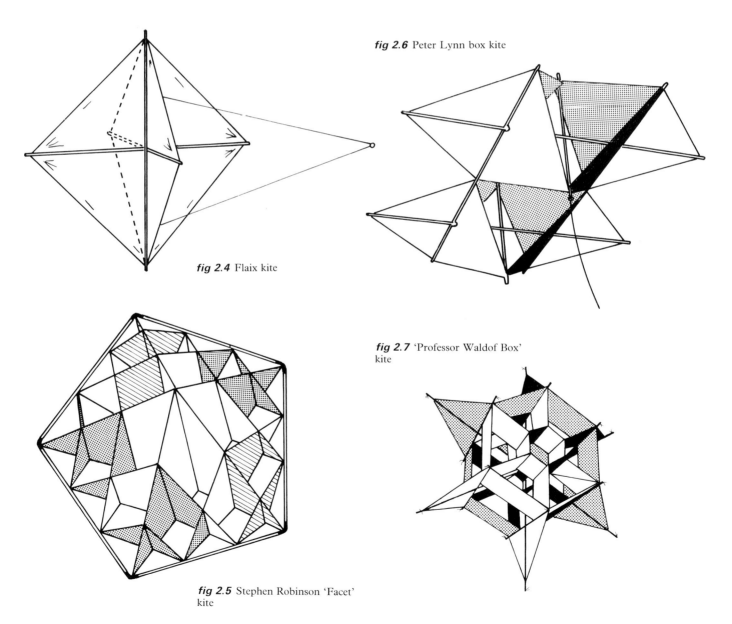

fig 2.4 Flaix kite

fig 2.6 Peter Lynn box kite

fig 2.5 Stephen Robinson 'Facet' kite

fig 2.7 'Professor Waldof Box' kite

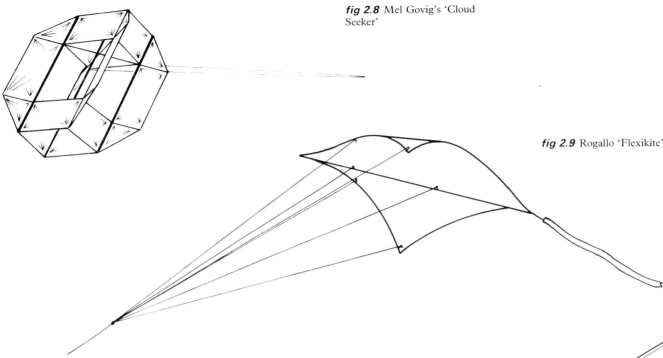

fig 2.8 Mel Govig's 'Cloud Seeker'

fig 2.9 Rogallo 'Flexikite'

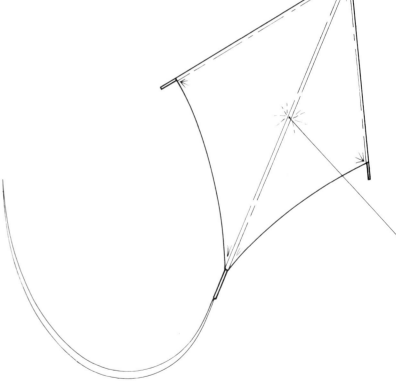

Mel Govig's 'Cloud Seeker' (Fig 2.8) seems at first to be yet another variation on the standard winged box but, for reasons which I find difficult to explain, it has captured the imagination of a number of home constructors. Cloud Seekers, particularly in trains, are seen frequently at festivals lifting everything from teddy bears to coloured flares, although I've yet to see it stunted as Mel suggests it can!

The latest range of boxes, coming mainly from American designers, Red Braswell, Kathy Goodwind and Tom Mallard, are described as 'tumbling' kites which can be made to toss and tumble through controlled line tension. While the concept of a tumbling kite is not new, its application to these high aspect-ratio facet derivatives, to show off the kite's colour and shape is quite fascinating, although more an entertainment for the spectator than the flier, I suspect!

DELTA KITES

Unlike the box kite, whose invention is, perhaps wrongly, attributed to the work of one person, the modern delta is the product of an evolution spanning sixty years.

In 1911 an otherwise unknown, Ferdinand Lischtiak, filed a patent for a bird kite in which the leading edges were not fixed but able to pivot freely about the tip, the basic delta principle. His kite was never manufactured commercially, however.

Some forty years later, aeronautical engineer Francis Rogallo developed a kite consisting of a flexible, diamond-shaped wing divided into two conical sections. His aim was to produce a design with the stability of a parachute and the lift of an aeroplane wing. The 'Flexikite' achieved both. It was light, flexible and efficient without any rigid support, but held in shape through the pressure of the wind and numerous bridles (Fig 2.9).

fig 2.10 'Glite'

One of the main patents derived from Rogallo's Flexikite was that of Charles Cleveland for North Pacific Product's 'Glite' (Fig 2.10). Here again the sail was diamond-shaped, but with rigid spars fitted along the spine and leading edges, all held in shape by a rigid plastic tip. With a sail made in polythene, it was also the first kite available in Britain that I recall being manufactured by modern mass-production techniques.

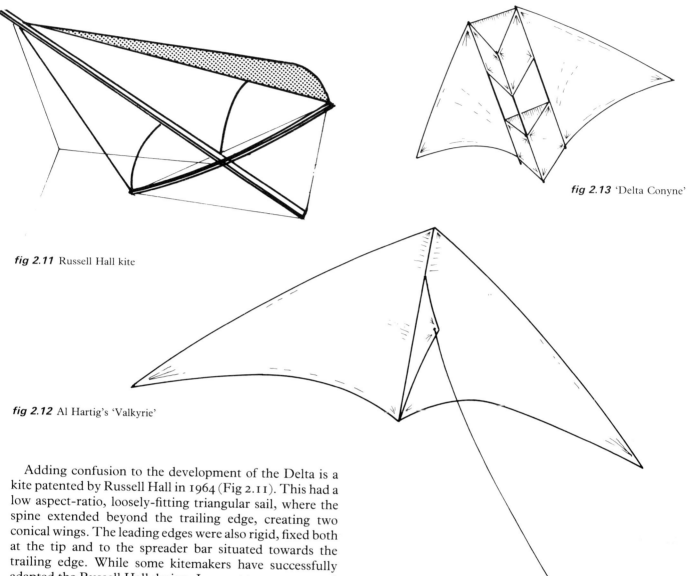

fig 2.13 'Delta Conyne'

fig 2.11 Russell Hall kite

fig 2.12 Al Hartig's 'Valkyrie'

Adding confusion to the development of the Delta is a kite patented by Russell Hall in 1964 (Fig 2.11). This had a low aspect-ratio, loosely-fitting triangular sail, where the spine extended beyond the trailing edge, creating two conical wings. The leading edges were also rigid, fixed both at the tip and to the spreader bar situated towards the trailing edge. While some kitemakers have successfully adapted the Russell Hall design, I cannot trace any record of it being produced commercially.

Although the name 'Delta' had long been used to describe a Rogallo wing with a rigid spine and leading edges, it was not until 1966 that the modern form of Delta kite finally emerged in a design by Al Hartig called the 'Valkyrie'. Here again the sail was triangular with rigid supports along the spine and leading edges (Fig 2.12). The latter were not fixed at the tip, however, but allowed to move freely, independently of each other and of the spine. To maintain the shape, a horizontal spreader bar was introduced to the rear of the sail, fixed at about one third of the length of the leading edge from the tip, while a forward triangular keel provided both a convenient point of attachment and a most efficient means of achieving lateral stability.

Al Hartig's design had many faults. Although the Valkyrie rose swiftly in an increasing gust, it had a tendency to pitch forward as the wind dropped again, and in an attempt to overcome this problem a flexible apron, later with serrations, was fitted along the trailing edge.

The size, shape and position of the keel was also found to be significant in creating a kite that would be stable in a variety of wind conditions, and several designers gave their attention to Delta improvements. One of the first was Ed Grauel with his 'Open Keel' delta, which possessed a forward keel made up of a narrow triangular cone with its apex at the trailing edge. The design proved to be very buoyant, undisturbed by gusts, but as far as I can tell never became very popular.

Martin Powell's 'Tunnel Keel' delta also makes use of a triangular cone, not to the front, as with previous designs, but to the rear with its apex at the tip. In flight the spine is pulled forward to create a three-dimensional keel open at the base. Whereas this innovation improved stability only marginally, it did, on the other hand, bring to the design an elegance and beauty which the simple triangular shape longed for.

Taking the concept of the three-dimensional triangular keel one stage further, designers such as Carol Masters, Curtis Marshall and John White have combined the box shape of the Conyne with the flexible wings of the Delta, to produce strange but very efficient hybrids (Fig 2.13).

While some designers worked to create an efficient stabilising keel, others sought to eliminate it altogether. Ed Grauel's 'Flapper', with its short, drag-inducing apron, was one of the first 'keelless' deltas, but perhaps those by Takeshi Nishbayashi, introduced in a book published in 1978, were the more successful, even though they had to compensate by adding tails and vents.

The improvements introduced by Helen Bushell are particularly interesting. In her 'Trefoil' delta the triangular keel is removed and the spine brought forward, to create a keel with a rigid leading edge. Furthermore, the rear junction of the keel and the two wings is not straight, but curved in a cambered aerofoil shape which she claims significantly improves its flying characteristics. Trefoils are, however, very dependent on the qualities of both sail and spar materials, and few home constructors have been particularly successful with them.

As well as the size, shape and construction of the keel, designers have also been experimenting with different wing shapes. Of the low aspect-ratio designs, Bob Quinlivan's Japanese-inspired square delta must rank as the strangest I've encountered, while at the other extreme Bill Lee's high aspect-ratio, scalloped-wing kites have to be the most graceful.

In all the previous designs, the two wing tips and the base of the spine form a straight line, which naturally suggests two other wing shapes: one where the spine base is above the line joining the two wing tips (extended wing); and one where it is below this line (clipped wing).

Clipped-wing deltas are generally quite unstable, but Dan Leigh's 'Balloon Keel Delta' also features a keel made of two layers of fabric open at the leading edge, which billows out in the wind to create a conical stabilising tube (Fig 2.14). Dan has a fine reputation for both the design and construction of deltas, fully justified in this kite, which is in my view his finest.

Finally, let me introduce a real monster of a kite by Ted Fleming (Fig 2.15). Notoriously difficult to make, the 'Ram Delta' is, on the other hand, an extremely efficient and stable flier and features a high aspect-ratio, battened, scalloped sail; a forward dihedralled spreader bar; three stabilising 'rams' to the rear and, with the latest versions, a short tail. Follow that!

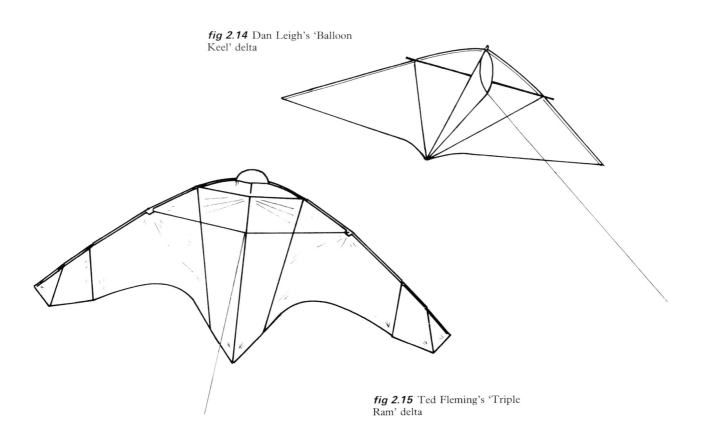

fig 2.14 Dan Leigh's 'Balloon Keel' delta

fig 2.15 Ted Fleming's 'Triple Ram' delta

STUNTER KITES

Stunters are not a true kite family with a unique configuration, but have evolved somewhat independently of other kites and so it will be useful to consider them as such.

Despite the impression of being a very recent phenomenon, stunter kites, or, as they are more correctly known, 'two-line dirigible kites' are not particularly new and have been flown in China for possibly thousands of years. They did not appear in the West, however, until the 1890s.

Some forty years later navy commander Paul Garber developed what was so aptly named the 'Target' kite. Essentially an Eddy kite with a rudder and control bar, it was flown for target practice by US soldiers during World War II.

Probably the first of the new generation of control-line kites was the 'Flying Machine', designed by Don Dunford in the 1960s (Fig 2.16). In appearance it resembled the Conyne, with a forward longeron and triangular wings, but removal of the rear face of the box triangle and careful selection of the sail fabric created a highly manoeuvrable and very popular kite.

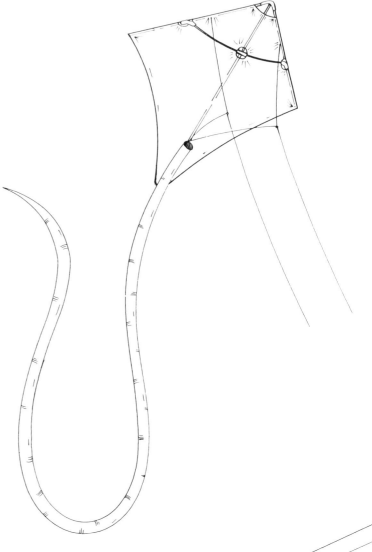

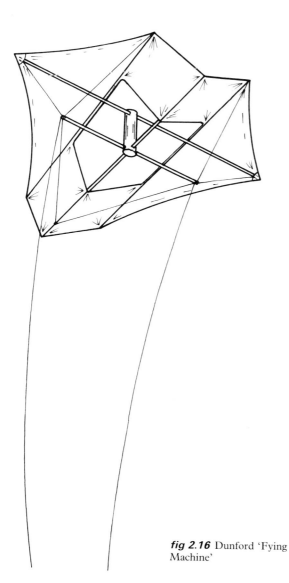

fig 2.16 Dunford 'Flying Machine'

fig 2.17 Peter Powell stunter kite

'Stunters' are, however, more closely associated with the name Peter Powell. Peter took the standard Rogallo Flexikite sail and instead of introducing a rigid moulded tip, as in the Glite, created a simple flexible tip together with a forward, sprung spreader bar. Another unique feature of the Powell stunter, and one of the reasons for its outstanding success, was the long, brightly-coloured tubular tail which created beautiful flowing patterns in the wake as the kite was manoeuvred. It was cheap, strong, reliable, easy to fly and at the time the most exciting kite to be found (Fig 2.17).

The 'Flexifoil', developed by Ray Merry and Andrew Jones, is a unique variation on the more usual stunter: not a member of the delta/Malay families but a parafoil, in which the sail is made up of a number of cambered aerofoil cells inflated by the wind (Fig 2.18). Control lines are attached to the ends of a flexible spar along the leading edge, and it is manoeuvred with the assistance of a stiff control bar. Flexifoils are highly efficient designs in relation to both power and manoeuvrability and, whistling through the sky at great speed, they can be great fun to fly.

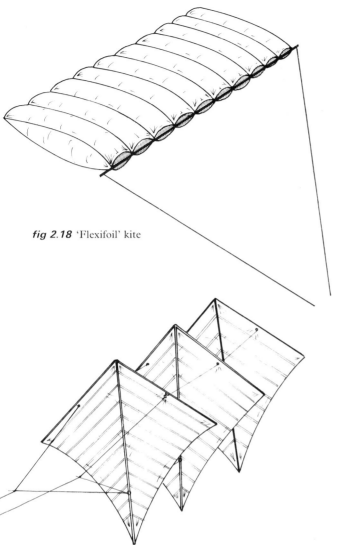

fig 2.18 'Flexifoil' kite

Not quite a Malay nor an Indian fighter, Max Puckridge's 'Ace' features a diamond-shaped polythene sail with a fibreglass spine and bowed horizontal spar (Fig 2.19). Like the Peter Powell stunter, the main reasons for its success were simple construction, low price and effective marketing.

Steve Edeiken's 'Rainbow', on the other hand, utilises the form of the Peter Powell, but is much smaller, stronger and made specifically for flying in a stack. The tip is also made from sprung steel, with spars of alloy tube and a sail of lightweight rip-stop nylon. Although Rainbows have sold widely in the United States and Europe, they have not been particularly popular in Britain.

With the pursuit of world records in mind, some designers have started to give their attention to miniature stunter kites. Rick Bell's 'Hyperkite', for example, is a delta with a forward spreader bar and pivoting spine, specifically designed to be flown in a stack (Fig 2.20). Miniature Flexifoils of barely 60 cm span have also been produced.

The newest stunters come from the United States and are the work of Don Tabor and Tony Cyphert. The 'Hawaiian' and 'Avenger' feature chevron-shaped sails in multi-coloured rip-stop which can be tuned to respond, quickly and accurately to very light control (Fig 2.21).

As well as their high manoeuvrability, unequalled by any other design, these kites have brought with them a new concept – close formation aerobatics in which teams of fliers standing side by side present displays of synchronised, controlled flying. Team flying is at present an American phenomenon, coming only slowly to Europe, but in doing so is creating a new enthusiasm amongst kite clubs, all eager to show off their skill and professionalism.

fig 2.19 'Ace' stunter kite

fig 2.21 'Avenger' stunter kites

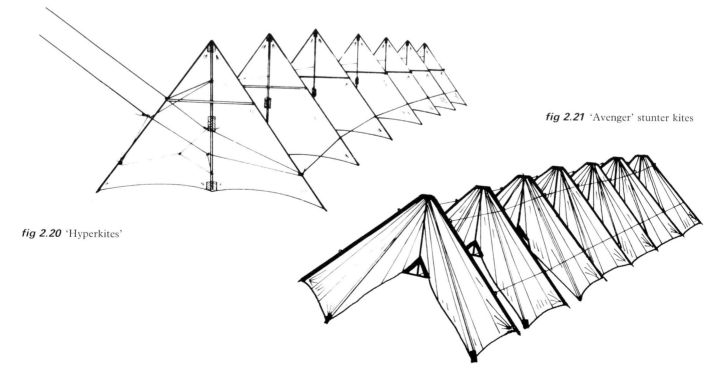

fig 2.20 'Hyperkites'

SLEDS

While Francis Rogallo was busy creating his 'Flexikite', fellow American William Allison was hard at work developing another flexible kite. The 'Sled', as it later became known, was the ultimate in simplicity, consisting of a flat, six-sided sail with three vertical spars (Fig 2.22). A most unlikely configuration, but fly it most certainly did.

Despite its simplicity, or perhaps because of it, the sled has captured the attention of a good many designers. Frank Scott, who was responsible for much of the kite's early popularity, removed the central spar, setting the remaining two parallel, while also adding a triangular-shaped vent (Fig 2.23).

Even with Scott's improvements, the sled still had a tendency to collapse as the wind dropped and 'wobble' as the air-flow was shed alternately to each side. In order to cure particularly the latter of these two problems, Ed Grauel introduced two trapezoidal vents in place of Scott's single vent.

Guy Aydlett, on the other hand, turned his attention to the problem of collapse and the 'Hornbeam' sled features a curved, rather than straight, leading edge, but without vents (Fig 2.24).

One of the more interesting improvements to the sled comes again from Ed Grauel. The 'Bullet' features two semicircular tubes to the rear of the sail which overcome the problems of both wobble and collapse. But this additional stability is only achieved at the expense of flying-angle, and the Bullet will not usually fly above 60–70 degrees. Perhaps for this reason, it has not been terribly popular amongst enthusiasts.

In 1978 a new sort of sled started to appear. Designed by Richard Lewis, the 'Flexible Pocket Kite' was sparless, with two conical tubes to the rear of the sail which helped retain the shape and provide stability. It was light, neat, simple and extremely portable – the ultimate pocket kite (Fig 2.25).

Often overlooked are the very strange sleds of Takeshi Nishbayashi, introduced in his book published in 1978. Wherever he goes Nishi wears a badge inscribed with the words *Tako Kichi* (Kite Crazy), which is a pretty accurate description of his personality. But crazy or not, the simplicity and effectiveness of his kites, such as 'Tubular Sled', 'Siamese Sled' and 'Elephant Sled', are not to be under-estimated.

Unlike many other designs, which also have more serious applications, the sled remains a toy. But its simplicity, both in geometric form and construction, make it a very popular design, and as a first kite to make and fly there is none finer.

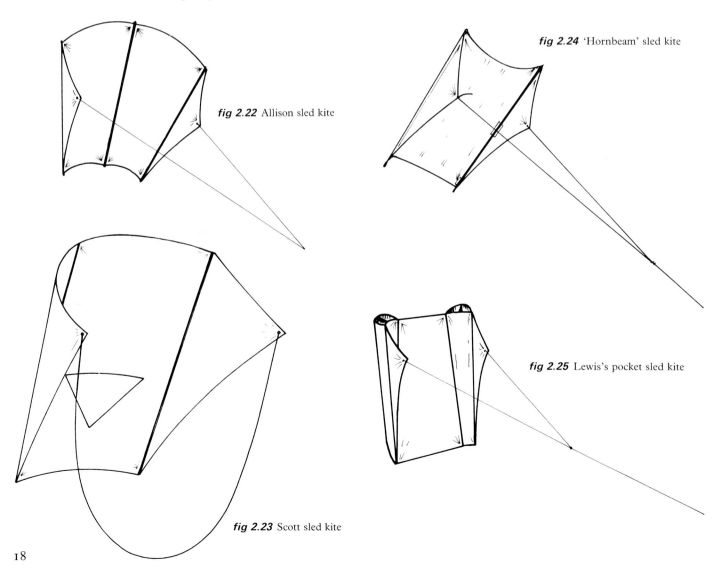

fig 2.24 'Hornbeam' sled kite

fig 2.22 Allison sled kite

fig 2.25 Lewis's pocket sled kite

fig 2.23 Scott sled kite

PARAFOILS

The youngest of the kite families, the parafoils, derives from the work of French-Canadian designer, Domina Jalbert. Jalbert spent much of his time refining the design of parachutes and aerial lifting devices, and by the 1960s already had several patents to his name. Like Rogallo, he appreciated the role of the wind in creating form in a kite, and the aim of his design was to produce a lifting surface which, when inflated by the wind, formed a low-speed aerofoil. The result was a wing consisting of a number of closed cells separated by aerofoil-shaped risers. To maintain stability, small fins or 'ventrals' were sewn to the lower surface and the whole canopy held in shape by a large number of bridles or 'shrouds' (Fig 2.26).

The idea of closing the leading edge completely and introducing air via valves on the lower surface was first postulated by Bob Ingraham in an article in the magazine *Kite Tales*, published in 1970. Sean Rawnsley was probably the first British designer to use this principle in his strange-looking 'Paraflate' (Fig 2.27). But better known, perhaps, are Dave Green's 'Stratoscoops' which feature intake valves just behind the leading edge (Fig 2.28).

Steven Sutton's 'Flowform' is a more unusual refinement of the basic parafoil in which 'pressure flow vents' are introduced between the cells and on the surfaces of the kite.

The aerofoil section is also extremely deep in comparison to other designs, and the central part of the trailing edge is left unsewn. Consequently, instead of the air flowing against and around the aerofoil cells, as with standard parafoils, the air flows through them, creating a kite capable of flying over a much wider range of wind speeds but generally at a lower angle of elevation.

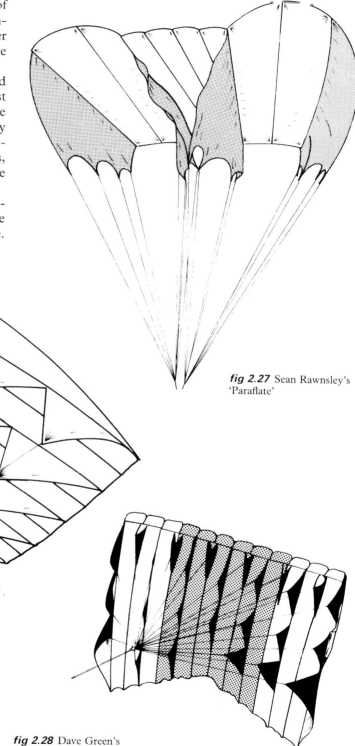

fig 2.27 Sean Rawnsley's 'Paraflate'

fig 2.26 Parafoil

fig 2.28 Dave Green's 'Stratoscoop'

WINDSOCK KITES

Overlooked for centuries, windsock kites are slowly gaining in popularity, not only because of a greater understanding of Eastern kitelore but also the innovative flair of a small number of designers.

Martin Lester, for example, has introduced a range of semi-rigid inflatable kites in both original and imaginative shapes: 'Space Shuttle', 'Shark', 'Icarus the Flying Man' and a whole flock of birds, each created with the accuracy and detail of the original (Fig 2.29).

ROTOR KITES

Rotors are aerodynamically different from other designs and, to generate a lifting force, depend not on the action of the wind against the kite but on their spinning motion.

Sadly, few designers have given much serious attention to these kites and most have been manufactured as children's toys. Guy Aydlett is possibly the most well-known and the acknowledged 'expert', but his designs, although aerodynamically superior to others, are difficult to make

and demand a degree of engineering skill beyond that of most enthusiast kitemakers.

Stanley Albertson's 'Rotoki', consisting of two 'S'-section wings with stabilising discs at each end, enjoyed a short spell of popularity in the early 1970s, principally in the United States. Except for a number of enthusiast copies, however, few were seen in Britain (Fig 2.30). Other rotors based on the basic 'H' shape of the Rotoki have also appeared from time to time, but none achieved any degree of success either as toys or amongst the kite fraternity.

Now regarded as the 'classic' rotor, the design patented by Ken Sams in 1962 features an 'S'-section elliptical wing, free to turn about its long axis, together with a centrally-placed stabilising disc. It was manufactured in the 1970s under various names but, like the Rotoki, was quite fragile and not a great commercial success. It was, on the other hand, very easy to make and enthusiast copies are regularly seen at festivals.

In 1978 Ken patented a second, more robust, rotor, made from *Mylar* on a fibreglass frame, but which retained the elliptical wing and stabilising disc. The 'Ufosam' has only recently become available, however, launched in a blaze of publicity, and its success has been more as a novelty toy for children than as an enthusiast's kite.

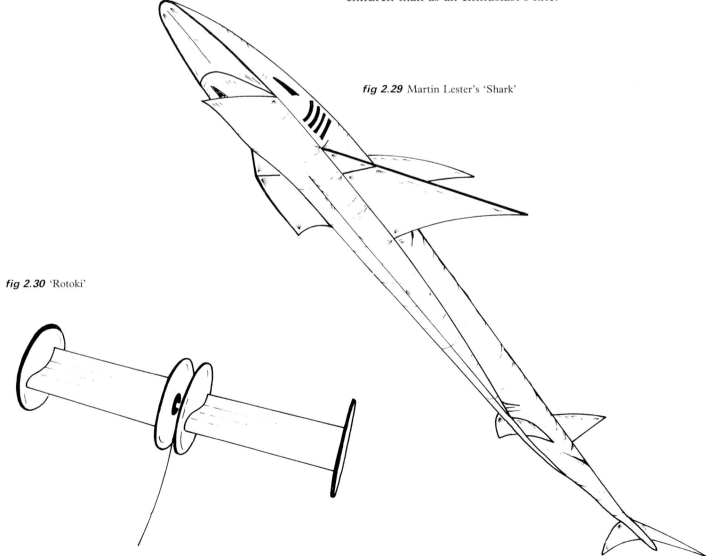

fig 2.29 Martin Lester's 'Shark'

fig 2.30 'Rotoki'

CHAPTER THREE

kitemaking materials

Part of the fun of making your own kites is to use materials immediately to hand, such as supermarket shopping-bags, garden canes, newspaper and wrapping paper, all of which can make very enjoyable kites. As your skills develop, however, you may wish to broaden your approach, and in this chapter we assess the qualities of a range of materials which you might consider.

SAILS

Irrespective of the size, shape or configuration of your kite, its performance, how high or how stable it flies and how easily it responds to control is determined almost wholly by qualities of the sail materials. Not only must you consider factors such as weight and strength, but also flexibility, porosity and, in the case of fabrics, the amount and direction they will stretch. These latter qualities are particularly important in relation to flexible kites such as sleds, deltas and parafoils.

Paper

While obviously limited in strength and durability, paper can be used very successfully for kitemaking and is of course the traditional sail material of many kitemaking cultures, principally China and Japan.

The range of papers available to the oriental kitemaker is not, however, as easily obtainable elsewhere and enthusiasts consequently make use of tissue, greaseproof, art paper, wrapping paper or even wallpaper, all of which can be used to great effect.

Washi, a traditional Japanese paper, can be purchased in Britain from one or two specialist dealers, but you will have to search long and hard to find others such as *Takamatsu* or *Yoshino*.

Tissue paper can be purchased from retail stationers as A2 or A3 sized sheets in a wide range of colours. It is light, easy to shape and will accept a range of adhesives, but is neither terribly strong nor waterproof. Its use is consequently restricted to kites made using traditional string frame techniques.

Silkspan, or as it is known in Britain, *Modelspan*, is the tissue paper used by model aircraft enthusiasts for wing and fuselage coverings. It is light, slightly waterproof, and both stronger and more durable than standard tissue. Most model shops will stock it in a small range of thicknesses, but usually only in white.

Synthetic papers

Although used at present by only a small number of manufacturers, synthetic papers are slowly becoming available to the home kitemaker. They are made by coating a thin polymer film, such as polypropylene or polystyrene, with a surface emulsion to allow printing. Opaque and usually white in colour, synthetic papers are also light, strong and resistant to both stretching and tearing.

Although some Japanese synthetics can be purchased from specialist importers, *Synteape*, a multiply polypropylene from Wiggins Teape Ltd, is perhaps the most widely available in Britain. It is extremely strong, and stretches little, but if punctured or cut it will tear easily. *Synteape* will also accept a wide range of colours, including acrylic paints, spirit-based felt-tip pens and a variety of adhesives.

Du Pont *Tyvek* is a very different type of synthetic paper altogether. It is made not as a coated film but from very long polymer fibres overlaid in a random pattern to produce a strong, paper-like material, resistant to both stretching and tearing.

Two forms of *Tyvek* are generally available. Type 10 looks, feels and can be treated like paper but is more durable and, most important, doesn't disintegrate when wet. Type 14 is softer, more flexible, handles more like a fabric and is slightly porous. Both *Tyveks* can be glued or sewn and will accept water and some spirit-based colours. Kite stores vary in the stock they normally supply, but Type 10 is perhaps the easier to obtain.

Polythene

Polythene is a very popular kitemaking material, particularly among newcomers without access to a sewing machine and, of course, for kitemaking workshops. It is light, cheap, often brightly coloured and available in a wide range of weights and forms. Dustbin liners, for example, in black or white from supermarkets or in green from garden centres, are ideal for kite sails, as are polythene shopping bags.

If, on the other hand, you plan to make extensive use of polythene, it may pay you to buy a whole roll. A glance through the telephone Yellow Pages should reveal a couple of local suppliers. By shopping around, it is also possible to buy rolls or roll ends, of single colours, but do be careful about the weight and thickness. Anything less than 100 gauge is really not strong enough for kites, while above 600 gauge is too heavy.

Despite its wide availability, polythene does have a number of disadvantages: it cannot be glued, although single or double-sided adhesive tape can be used and some of the heavier polythenes can be welded; it is not particularly strong; it stretches and punctures easily; and lastly, without treatment the surface does not accept inks or paints.

Polypropylene
Polypropylene is similar in many respects to polythene and available in many of the same forms, such as supermarket bags and 'bin' liner bags. It is, however, stronger, lighter, and less prone to stretching than polythene of equivalent thickness, but unfortunately tears more easily.

Polyester films
Mylar is a lightweight polyester film produced by Du Pont. It is extremely strong, resistant to both stretching and tearing and is used extensively for commercial kite manufacture.

Unfortunately for British kitemakers, all *Mylar* is imported and a local supplier will be almost impossible to find. Kite stores do occasionally have small stocks, but usually only in clear or silver, sold at about the same price as *Tyvek*.

The ICI equivalent to *Mylar* is *Melinex*, manufactured in a wide range of surface finishes and thicknesses. Kite stores rarely stock *Melinex*, and supplies should be sought from plastics wholesalers. A stockist should not be difficult to find, but you should be prepared to buy a whole roll, which may work out to be quite expensive.

The best source I have found for small quantities of *Melinex* is the specialist drawing-office supplier. Types 542 and 377 are translucent films which are pretreated to accept adhesives or colours, making them very suitable for kites.

Expanded polystyrene (Styrofoam)
Expanded polystyrene is a strange material made up of lightweight pellets joined together. Its more usual application is as packing or thermal insulation, but it can be used to a very limited degree in kitemaking.

Probably the best source of supply is the DIY store, where it can be purchased in 6 mm ($\frac{1}{4}$ inch) thick sheets (ceiling tiles) or 2 mm ($\frac{1}{8}$ inch) thick rolls (wall insulation). Expanded polystyrene is light, slightly porous, easy to cut and accepts a range of adhesives, but is neither particularly strong nor flexible.

Rip-stop nylon
'Rip-stop' is the name given to a range of closely-woven nylon fabrics with a weave of larger diameter thread superimposed on to the base weave in order to increase their strength and tear resistance. They were originally developed for parachutes during the 1940s as a substitute for silk, but are now manufactured for a wide range of applications, principally balloons, leisure wear, and as sailcloth.

For kitemaking purposes, balloon and spinnaker quality rip-stops are the most suitable. They are light: 20–60 g/sq. metre ($\frac{1}{2}$–2 oz/sq. yd); extremely strong, produced in a startling array of colours and, most important, are coated with a thin layer of polyurethane or PVC to reduce porosity.

Heavier rip-stops, 60–100 g/sq. metre (2–4 oz/sq. yd), can be used with some success, especially on kites with large sail areas. They are also particularly useful for making spar pockets or sail reinforcing. But beginners should avoid uncoated fabrics as they are very difficult to sew.

Seconds quality rip-stop, most often used for kitemaking, is in constant short supply and enthusiasts are regularly faced with little choice in weight or only a small range of colours. Perhaps the most reliable sources are the kite stores themselves, who generally have a fair stock, but because of supply difficulties you will still experience variations in weight and quality.

Other fabrics
There are probably many other fabrics which can be used successfully in kitemaking, but for brevity I shall consider just two: nylon/terylene taffetas and polycotton.

Close weave fabrics in nylon, terylene or polycotton can be purchased from most textile retailers in a fair range of colours and at moderate prices. They are on the whole light, 60–80 g/sq. metre (2–3 oz/sq. yd), and almost as strong as rip-stop, but some nylons and terylenes do have a tendency to stretch.

Although these fabrics lose over rip-stop in terms of weight, they are finding favour with a number of kitemakers purely because of their marginally increased porosity, which can on some designs improve stability.

SPARS

The second vital key to successful kitemaking is your choice of spar material. Again weight is an important factor, but also flexibility versus rigidity, strength and hardness needs to be considered.

Bamboo
Bamboo has, of course, been used for kite spars for thousands of years, particularly in regions where it grows naturally. It is light, cheap, quite strong and flexible. But unfortunately the skills of cane splitting, trimming and balancing are only learnt through precise instruction and long hard practice, and bamboo is usually reserved for more traditional designs where 'modern' materials would be either unsuitable or inappropriate.

If, however, your intention is to make a large number of kites, in a train for example, where cost is the overriding factor, then pre-split bamboo can be purchased from garden centres. Such canes are not, unfortunately, sufficiently reliable for general kitemaking.

Dowel
For modern designs, hardwood (Ramin) dowel, in diameters from 3 mm ($\frac{1}{8}$ inch) to 15 mm ($\frac{5}{8}$ inch), is the more popular material and may be purchased from a wide range of outlets such as DIY stores and model shops. If you can

find them, dowels in beech, birch, maple, ash, spruce and pine are also suitable.

Apart from their wide availability, dowels are light, cheap, relatively strong and of even section, while also possessing the right degree of rigidity for kite construction.

Since die-drawn dowels, particularly Ramin and the softwoods, tend to contain imperfections, it will pay you to choose them very carefully. While it is unlikely that you will come across many perfectly straight pieces, those in which the grain twists along the length or contain knots should be rejected.

Some kitemakers, rather than choosing pre-cut dowels, prefer to trim their own spars from square or rectangular sections of timber, in a manner not far removed from the traditional Eastern techniques. But, as with bamboo, the skills required cannot be learned overnight, and only come after an awful lot of practice.

Glass-reinforced plastics

Probably the most significant developments in kite design over the last ten years have come through the wider availability of glass-reinforced plastics – fibreglass. Previously only manufactured in the form of tapered fishing rod blanks, GRP can now be purchased in tubes or rods in diameters from 1 mm ($\frac{1}{32}$ inch) upwards, principally from kite stores.

Fibreglass has two very useful properties in the eyes of the kitemaker. Firstly it is so strong as to be almost unbreakable. Spars will consequently accept very rough handling and numerous crashes without any apparent damage. It is also very flexible, and fibreglass is slowly taking the place of bamboo in modern variations of traditional designs.

Flexibility is also its greatest drawback, however. In many kites rigid, inflexible spars are required and in this respect fibreglass is a poor second to dowel. Kites designed for dowel spars rarely perform as well with fibreglass as substitute, since not only are they much heavier, but the relative position of the centre of gravity is also changed, drastically altering their flying characteristics.

Fibreglass is also very hard and unforgiving, and special attention must be given to the shape, strength and position of spar end pockets.

Alloy tube

On large kites, particularly boxes above 2–3 metres (6–9 feet) in span, none of the above materials is sufficiently strong or rigid to hold the sail in shape, and in such cases most designers would normally turn to alloy tube.

It can be purchased in a range of wall thicknesses and diameters from non-ferrous metal merchants, but is of course quite expensive. There is also such a vast array of lightweight alloys available that some fairly detailed investigation of stress and sail loading must be made before you can even begin to select the correct material.

KITE-LINE

More serious kitefliers spend as much time selecting their kite-line as they would a sail or spar material. Strength is of course the most important factor, but a line which stretches will make flying difficult, perhaps impossible, while one which deteriorates in water or sunlight obviously won't last very long.

Kite-line is usually described in terms of its breaking strain – the tension it will support before breaking, expressed as so many pounds or kilos. But remember this is a maximum value and it will actually break at about a quarter of this amount. Knots, either within the line or at the ends, will also significantly weaken it.

Before selecting a line it is useful to calculate how much force the wind will exert against the kite. Obviously this will vary from design to design, flat kite or box kite, and the wind speed, but as a rough guide, you can use a simple 'sail factor'. If you prefer metric units this factor is 20–20 kg breaking strain per square metre of sail area; in Imperial units it is 5–5 lb breaking strain per square foot of sail.

For example, a standard square box kite with a 30 cm (12 inch) square sail would require a line of

30 cm (12 in) × 30 cm (12 in) × 8 sails = 0.72 sq. metres
(8 sq ft)
= 15 kg (40 lb)
breaking strain

Button thread

For smaller kites button thread, usually polyester, with a breaking strain of 2–5 kg (4–10 lb) is quite adequate and can be obtained both cheaply and easily from high-street haberdashery stores in small 50 m (150 feet) reels or sometimes in larger bobbins.

Linen/hemp twine

Until the arrival and general acceptance of nylon and polyester, kitefliers used linen or hemp twine almost exclusively. Even now, many older fliers still seek out supplies. Reliable sources are becoming increasingly difficult to find, however, and prices are accordingly quite high, but if natural line is what you prefer then your search will no doubt be worthwhile.

Monofilament line

Monofilament nylon fishing line (what anglers call pike, cod or shark line), having a breaking strain of 1–50 kg (1–100 lb), is quite suitable for kites. It is cheap, light, strong and widely available from fishing-tackle suppliers.

Narrower monofilament, however, tangles very easily, and if this happens your best course of action is to cut the line and throw it away – not on the kite field, though! With larger diameters the opposite problem occurs: they tangle less but are difficult to knot.

The most serious disadvantage of monofilament is its low resistance to abrasion and tendency to stretch. If your line gets caught or tangled the surface soon starts to wear, and you should check it carefully for abrasions after each flight.

Twisted industrial thread

For kites requiring breaking strains up to 20 kg (45 lb) twisted industrial sewing thread, made up of 2, 4, 6 or sometimes 8 individual strands in nylon or polyester, has taken the place of linen and hemp.

My own source is the local market, where bobbins of 1000 metres (3000 feet) can be bought quite cheaply. Kite stores will also supply a range of threads in various breaking strains.

Twisted thread does tend to unravel in time, however, and is prone to tangling. Alternatively, waxed thread manufactured for machine stitching suffers less from these sort of problems, but be very careful, as it will easily cut into an ungloved hand.

Braided industrial line – polyester and nylon

For higher breaking strains, 15 kg (35 lb) and above, polymer fibres are more usually braided to form a tube around a central circular or elliptical core.

Kite stores are probably the best source of supply of braided line, although yacht chandlers are more likely to have the higher breaking strains – 100 kg (200 lb) and above. Both will very often supply line by the metre or standard cop.

Dacron

Developed by Du Pont in the 1970s, *Dacron* is much stronger than standard polyester, has less tendency to stretch, and is especially suited for flying stunter kites.

Although it is used extensively in the United States and Europe, *Dacron* is much harder to find in bulk lengths in Britain, particularly in the lower range 20–150 kg (45–350 lb). The most likely source is the fishing tackle shop, where it is sold for making/tying underwater nets.

Kevlar

Kevlar is yet another fibre to come out of the Du Pont laboratories. It is light, exceptionally strong and does not stretch – ideal qualities for kite line, you might think. But the surface of raw *Kevlar* is very rough – so abrasive that it is impossible to knot.

Kevlar is also extremely dangerous. Its rough surface, combined with very narrow diameters, will cut through gloves and into hands without difficulty, and on a crowded kite field its use is unforgiveable.

Some principally American companies are making *Kevlar* available either within a braided sleeve or coated to reduce abrasion, but even in this form it should only be used with extreme care.

OTHER MATERIALS

PVC Tube

PVC tube is now used extensively in kitemaking, for creating flexible joints between spars, protecting spar ends, and for creating spar-sail connections.

It is available in a range of diameters, mainly in two forms: a clear thin-walled tube, which is light, very flexible and reasonably strong; and a thick-walled braided (hydraulic) tube, less flexible but obviously much stronger.

Both are quite cheap and widely available from model shops and plastics suppliers. The local beer or winemaking shop will also prove a useful source of 6 and 8 mm ($\frac{1}{4}$ inch – $\frac{5}{16}$ inch) diameter thin-walled PVC, where it is sold as siphon tubing.

Some stores will sell PVC tube by the metre, but it is more commonly available in standard lengths of 30 m (100 feet).

Metal tube

For the creation of a rigid joint – say at the centre of a long spar or at a dihedral – brass, steel or aluminium tube is most often used.

For spar diameters in the range 8–15 mm ($\frac{5}{16}$–$\frac{5}{8}$ inch), thick-walled 20–25 SWG (0.5–0.9 mm) aluminium alloy should provide a sufficiently strong and rigid joint. Such tubes are usually available through non-ferrous metal stockists, although possibly only to order. For smaller diameters, however, brass tube is stronger and easier to obtain from model shops.

Some kite stores also suply both brass and aluminium tube in a range of diameters.

Other plastics (PVC, Polypenkolene nylon, polycarbonate . . .)

The most common use of these plastics in kitemaking is for the creation of joints, on a multi-winged box kite for example, where the design demands that several spars be joined at various angles and in more than one plane. Their manufacture does, however, require access to a sophisticated workshop.

Another application of these plastics relates specifically to large kites utilising fibreglass spars. On such kites there can be so much pressure on the 'pocket' that the standard method of construction, utilising double layers of fabric, is far too weak, and the spar end cap should be made from a solid plastic rod.

Suitable rods can be purchased from general plastics suppliers, but usually only to order, especially in the smaller diameters 6–8 mm ($\frac{1}{4}$–$\frac{5}{16}$ inch).

Fabric tapes

Those making fabric kites will also need to arm themselves with a range of tapes.

The local haberdashery shop will usually have a range of tapes in various widths and colours, but do take care with your selection of materials. 'Bias binding', although widely available, is not at all suitable for kitemaking since it will stretch. You should instead choose a tape in polyester, or a polyester mix in a plain or twill weave with a width of 8–12 mm ($\frac{5}{16}$–$\frac{1}{2}$ inch). This will adapt to most applications, such as edge binding and for spar ties.

Although cotton tapes can be used for spar ties, you should avoid using them for edge binding as they will shrink and tighten, possibly distorting the shape of the sail.

Alternatively, tapes can be made from fabric scraps cut along the weave, folded twice and sewn along their length.

Thread

The selection of a suitable thread is one which many kitemakers fail to consider properly, if at all. It should of course be a polyester or polyester mix, but definitely *not* cotton, as this will shrink.

Your thread should also be strong enough to hold the kite together, under whatever strain the winds may impose, yet not so thick that it won't sew. Haberdashery stores will usually offer advice, but don't be tempted into buying large cheap bobbins without trying a sample first.

Swivels, rings and clips

Rings, clips and swivels are required for a number of applications in kitemaking.

Punched aluminium 'D' or 'O' rings in a range of diameters can be purchased quite cheaply from kite stores and camping shops.

For some applications, corner connections for example, nickel-plated split rings are preferable, and may be purchased in diameters from about 6 mm ($\frac{1}{4}$ inch), also quite cheaply from kite stores and fishing tackle suppliers.

The choice of a connection between the kite and the line varies tremendously. Some tie the line directly to the bridle ring, while others use a range of swivels and clips. 'American' snap swivels, the cheapest and most popular variety, may be purchased in a range of sizes from fishing tackle suppliers, but recently some kitefliers have been using swivels with ball bearings, claiming that these are more efficient. Views vary.

Heavier weight swivels of 50 kg (100 lb) and above can be purchased from yacht chandlers, although at this sort of weight it is more usual to tie the line direct.

Adhesives and adhesive tapes

Everybody has his or her own preference as to whether they use adhesives, and which types. I make extensive use of adhesives and usually have available in the workshop: a glue-stick (water-soluble for light paper kites); a can of aerosol adhesive; light glue paste (non-water-based, suitable for fabrics, heavier papers and Tyvek); electric glue gun; vinyl cement (will glue PVC); urea formaldehyde glue (Araldite) and an instant glue.

It is also useful to have a range of adhesive tapes. Celluloid tape (Sellotape) can be used with polythene, papers and Tyvek, and is available quite cheaply from stationers in a range of widths and colours. Double-sided Sellotape is not only useful for paper kites but also for holding sails in position during sewing.

Finally, a good supply of rip-stop tape, both in the workshop and out on the kite-field, is an absolute must. It can be used for reinforcing, making strong spar pockets, connecting towing and spar rings, quick repairs and a thousand other uses. Some kite stores sell rip-stop tape fairly cheaply, but it can also be made using fabric scraps and double-sided carpet tape.

A range of different kite lines: button thread, industrial sewing (twisted) thread, braided polyester line and Kevlar

construction techniques

As you develop your skills of kitemaking you will also become more familiar with the materials and construction methods. In this chapter we look at a range of techniques to help you get started, and which can of course be adapted to suit your own preference.

TOOLS

Kitemaking makes few demands in terms of tools, and the following should provide most of what you will need:

> Craft knife
> Scissors
> Metre rule/straight edge
> Junior hacksaw
> Hole punch
> Large set-square

> Those making fabric kites will also require:

> Hot cutting iron – a purpose-made sailmaker's iron
> Eyelets and eyelet pliers
> Domestic iron
> A sewing-machine! (Unless you want to hand sew)

It is also useful to arm yourself with a range of adhesives and adhesive tapes, particularly rip-stop tape.

MAKING THE SAIL

Templates

Kitemakers each have their own techniques for marking out the sail. Some draw directly on to the fabric: this can, however, leave unsightly construction marks. Others use tissue patterns not unlike those of the dressmaker. My own technique, used not only when teaching kitemaking but also in the workshop, is to cut around rigid templates.

Ideally the template should be of aluminium sheet, but the cost is not usually worthwhile unless you intend making kites by the hundred. For a single kite, therefore, a thin card or mounting board will provide a reasonably durable shape to mark or cut around.

Although they are time-consuming to make, the great advantage of templates is that they allow you to see how the various pieces fit together and can be most efficiently cut from the material. But do remember, particularly when using fabrics, to include within your template appropriate allowances for joins and hems.

Once you have made the templates and are ready to cut out, you will need a flat surface large enough to provide support all the way round. For example, I cut out on a large 1.5 m (5 feet) square piece of chipboard. It is also a good idea to *lightly* spray the cutting surface and the template with aerosol adhesive, the type graphic artists might use. This will increase friction between the surfaces and will help you keep them in position as you cut – particularly useful with rip-stop, which has a tendency to slither around.

The next stages vary, depending on whether you are using glued and welded materials, such as paper and polythene, or sewn fabrics.

Glued and welded materials

Cold cutting

A sharp craft knife, using the template as a straight edge, will provide the cleanest and most accurate cut on paper, polythene and Tyvek. But do be *very careful*, take your time, and keep your fingers away from the cutting edge (Fig 4.1).

In some situations, when working with children for example, it is not wise to have too many sharp knives about, and it is just as simple to mark around the template with a pencil, pen or tailor's chalk and cut out with scissors.

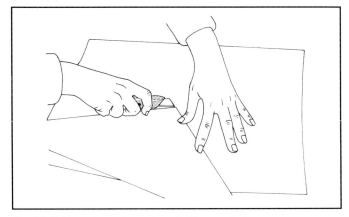

fig 4.1 Cold cutting using a sharp knife or scalpel

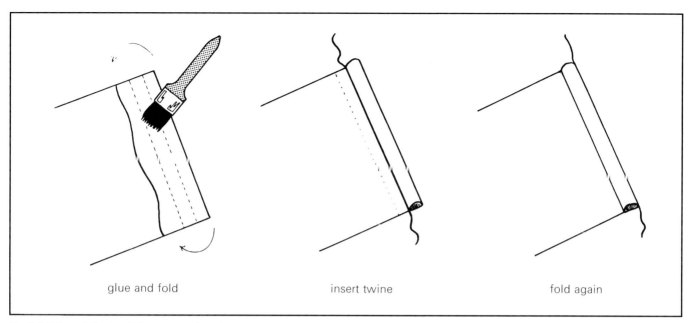

| glue and fold | insert twine | fold again |

fig.4.2 Edge reinforcing light papers using glue and twine

Edge reinforcing

Of the sail materials discussed earlier, only Tyvek 10 and the heavier polythenes are tough enough to survive without additional reinforcing, particularly on a fluttering trailing edge, and most will either puncture, tear or, more likely, fray.

The standard method of reinforcing light papers is to glue the edges in a double fold with a length of narrow twine in between (Fig 4.2).

With plastics, it is sufficient to reinforce the edges with Sellotape, lightweight vinyl tape, Mylar or polyester.

Joins

The simplest method of joining two pieces of paper is to overlap about 5 mm ($\frac{3}{16}$ inch) and glue. For a more instant join, however, adhesive tape can of course be used in a butt joint.

There are some designs in polythene where it is not possible to create an effective joint using adhesives or adhesive tapes and the only solution is to weld. In this case you will need a small domestic soldering iron, 15–25 watts, or purpose-made hand *polythene* welding iron, with a tip approx 1 mm ($\frac{1}{16}$ inch) in width.

Use a thin wooden (not metal) straight edge to guide the iron along the join to be created (Fig 4.3). Do remember, however, that, unlike joins using glue or tape, welded sail sections cannot be separated or adjusted later.

Sewn fabrics

It was only after making fabric kites for about two years that I felt I had started to get it right, so don't be too disappointed if your first efforts at sewing are less than perfect – just try again.

As you will find, all fabrics are not the same and each will demand a different thread, thread tension and stitch length which can only really be determined by trial and error. And even before attempting to make a kite, a few weeks' practice making seams and testing different stitches and thread

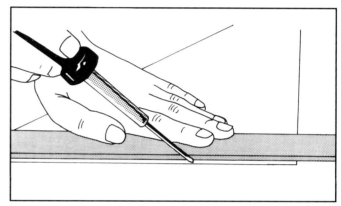

fig 4.3 Welding polythenes

tensions will save much disappointment and wasted fabric later.

You should aim to sew a neat seam which sits flat, not so tight that the fabric puckers and distorts, nor so loose that it pulls apart. Rip-stop, for example, will generally accept about 5–7 stitches per centimetre (12–14 per inch). Any more will weaken the fabric, any less will cause the sail to pucker as it comes under tension. Sometimes a zig-zag stitch is better, other times a straight stitch; much can only be learnt by experiment as you develop your own technique.

If, as you are sewing, you hear a constant 'popping' sound, then possibly the needle is too large. Change it for a narrower one or one with a different point. Random skipping of stitches, on the other hand, is a sure sign that the needle has not been fitted correctly or is too narrow. Again adjust or change it.

A thread which is constantly breaking can be a real annoyance, but should also be an indication that maybe the eye of the needle is too narrow, or that the thread is being pulled unevenly. Check the tension and make the necessary adjustments. It could also mean that your thread is of poor quality and should be found a better home in the waste bin.

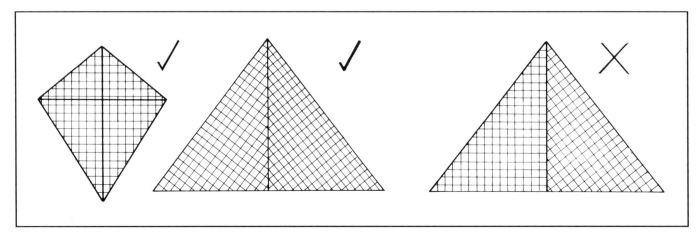

fig 4.4 You must ensure that the direction of the weave in symmetrical sail pieces is balanced

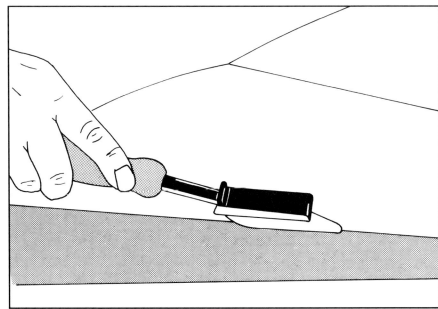

fig 4.5 Hot cutting of fabrics using a sailmaker's iron

Cutting out

When using fabrics, you should not only try to make the most efficient use of the materials but you also have to consider the weave. Fabrics are generally stronger and less prone to stretching in the direction of the weave, and a few moments' thought to consider the sail stresses will save hours of frustration out on the kite-field. Sometimes the weave should be parallel to the spine, sometimes parallel to the leading edge, but what you must *never* do is cut symmetrical pieces of sail with the weave in different directions (Fig 4.4).

With kites which have a large sail area, such as deltas, some improvement in performance can be achieved by making the sail from a number of fabric pieces, with the weave in differing directions, as with spinnaker yacht sails. But this method of construction calls for a lot of experimentation, observation and careful analysis of results, and is used by only a small number of professional kitemakers.

Both when cutting out and piecing sails together you should try to be as accurate as possible. Whereas most designs allow for a small margin of error in relation to dimensions, symmetrical sail pieces, on each wing of a delta for example, must be matched as exactly as possible, to an accuracy of o.1% if you can. This means that on a one-metre (39-inch) span kite the two wings must match to within 1 mm ($\frac{1}{16}$ inch).

Cold cutting

Fabrics may be cold cut with a knife in the manner described above, producing a clean accurate edge (not always possible using scissors). Sails cut in this way do, however, need to be reinforced at the edges to prevent fraying.

Hot cutting

Most fabrics can also be hot cut, sealing the edges, as an alternative to hemming or edge binding. If you prefer this method you are strongly advised to use a purpose-built sailmaker's cutting iron rather than an adapted soldering-iron. A purpose-built iron is more likely to be electrically safe, and will heat to the correct temperature for easy cutting (Fig 4.5).

Do also be aware that hot cutting can produce noxious fumes, particularly if you try to cut before the iron has reached its working temperature. And as a safety measure always ensure there is adequate ventilation.

Edge binding

Although edge binding is, in my experience, the more difficult method of reinforcing, it can also be made aesthetically pleasing when, for example, sail and binding are in contrasting colours. A second reason to prefer edge binding is in relation to curves, which cannot easily be hemmed without gathering the fabric.

To begin binding, make a crease along the first few centimetres of tape and gather it around the edge of the fabric, under the sewing foot (Fig 4.6) As you sew, carefully fold the tape, feeding it through evenly with the fabric. If your sewing-machine has a range of stitches, a zig-zag depth about 2–4 mm ($\frac{1}{8}$–$\frac{3}{16}$ inch) is possibly the better stitch to use, depending on the width of the tape.

Hemming

Hemming is either very easy or darn near impossible, depending on the fabric.

Being very crisp and light, spinnaker rip-stop stretches very little and can be creased in the hand. Making an accurate hem is therefore relatively simple. Lightly score a line 5 mm ($\frac{3}{16}$ inch) from the edge, fold, crease, then fold again to the final size and sew with a single straight or zig-zag stitch (Fig 4.7).

With softer rip-stops and other fabrics this is not as easy, since they will not accept a crease and will stretch, especially across the bias. Unless you are very careful the hemming process can pull the whole sail out of shape long before you've had a chance to get the kite in the air.

When using these softer fabrics, therefore, you will need to enlist the help of a cool iron. Mark the width of the hem, say 4–8 mm ($\frac{3}{16}$–$\frac{5}{16}$ inch), fold and crease using the iron, then as you sew, fold the fabric to the final size. Again a straight or zig-zag stitch can be used, as preferred.

On some sewing machines it is possible to fit a hem folding device, to either the foot or the baseplate. But in my experience such devices are not suited to rip-stop nylon since it slides around too much. They do, however, work very well with taffetas and polycottons.

On larger kites it may be necessary to reinforce the hems by sewing binding tapes within the hem fold, or on to the sail afterwards. The latter can be made to look particularly attractive. If you are undecided whether to hem or edge bind, here's a simple tip. If the majority of edges are parallel to the weave, then hem. If the majority of edges, particularly the leading edges, are cut across the bias, then bind.

fig 4.6 Edge-binding of fabrics. Fold the tape around the edge of the fabric and feed both evenly under the sewing-foot

fig 4.7 Fold and crease the edge of the spinnaker rip-stop by hand. As you sew fold again to the required size

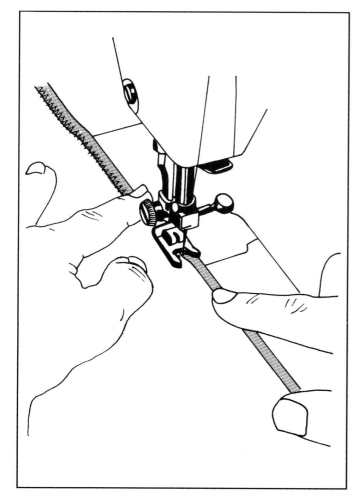

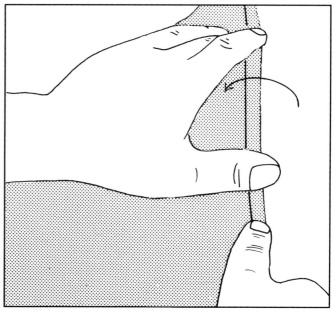

Joins

The easiest way to join two pieces of fabric is to use a plain seam (Fig 4.8 (a)). Lay the two pieces of fabric on top of one another, and sew a straight seam about 3 mm ($\frac{1}{8}$ inch) from the edge. To hold the pieces in position as you sew you can use either pins or double-sided tape. Also, don't be afraid to draw sewing lines on the fabric if you feel they will help you.

The plain seam is not too strong and limited in application, however. Instead, most kitemakers prefer the 'flat' or

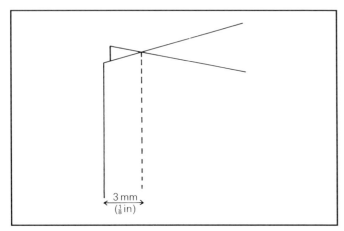

fig 4.8 (a) Plain seam

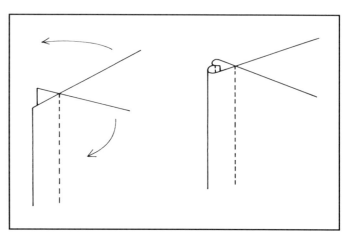

fig 4.8 (d) French seam

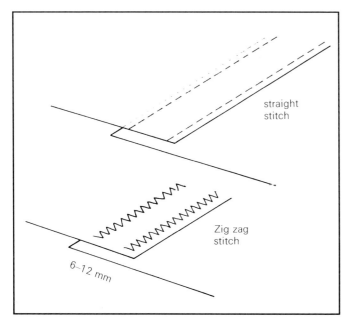

fig 4.8 (b) Flat or lap seam

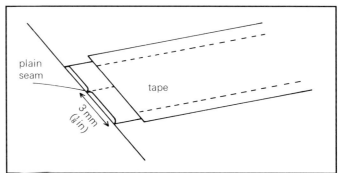

fig 4.8 (e) Notched seam

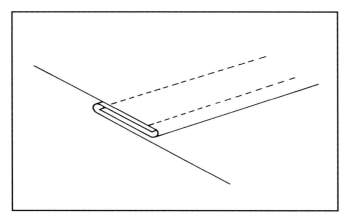

fig 4.8 (c) Double lap seam

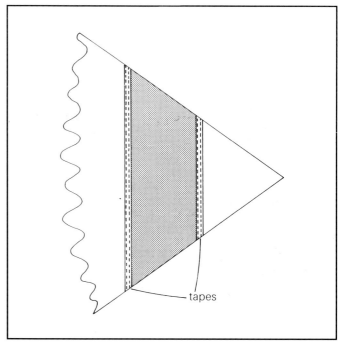

fig 4.9 Modular sail construction. Sail pieces are not sewn to each other but to narrow tapes

'lap' seam, Fig 4.8 (b), which, with two rows of zig-zag stitches, is neater, stronger, and can, more importantly, be sewn on curves. The 'double lap' or 'flat-fell' seam (Fig 4.8 (c)), on the other hand, is more often found on larger sails, especially where there is great stress. The 'French' (Fig 4.8 (d)) and 'notched' (Fig 4.8 (e)) seams are only occasionally used.

Another method of joining sail pieces has been described as 'modular' sail making. Here sail pieces are not joined to each other, but stitched to each side of a narrow tape (Fig 4.9). This method of construction is used with a number of corner and facet kites featured in later chapters.

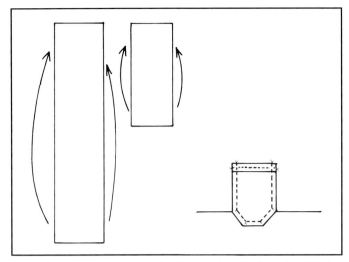

fig 4.10 Simple construction of a fabric pocket. Fold a strip of fabric at the centre, then fold it again. Fit and sew the pocket thus created to the edge of the sail

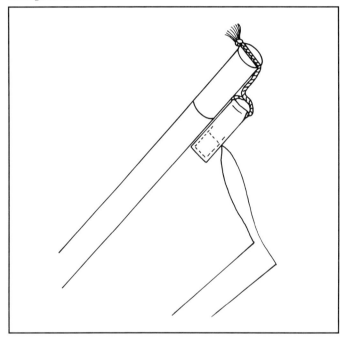

fig 4.11 (a) Knot and notch; used to hold longerons in place on box kites. Quite effective

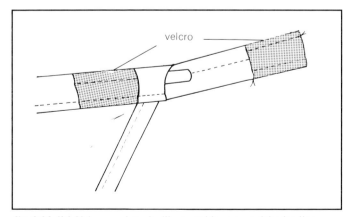

fig 4.11 (b) Velcro pocket. As illustrated here on a delta leading edge-spar but can also be used with box kite longerons, delta spines . . .

SPAR-SAIL CONNECTIONS

Strange as it may seem the design of the spar end-pocket can often mean the success or failure of a kite. Pockets should of course be strong, but should equally be fitted, such that the tension is spread as evenly as possible throughout the sail.

The simplest method of creating a spar pocket is to cut a small piece of fabric, fold it twice and sew in position (Fig 4.10). Other methods are illustrated in Figs 4.11 (a)–(j).

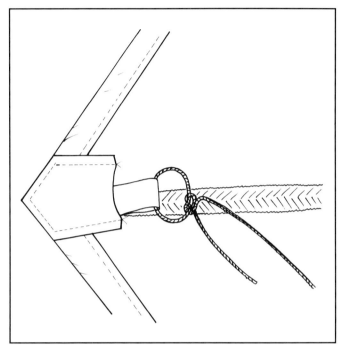

fig 4.11 (c) Standard double-fold pocket, here fitted with a loop for a bracing line

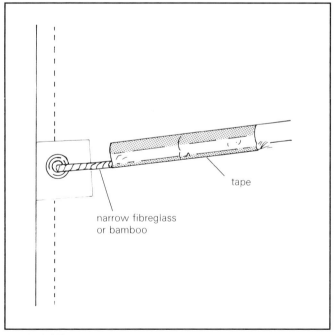

fig 4.11 (d) Spar and eyelet. Rarely used now since much stronger forms of connection have been developed

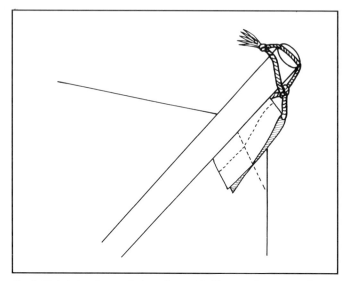

fig 4.11 (e) Another variation of 4.11 (a). Here used to secure the spine on a flat kite. Cheap and simple rather than effective

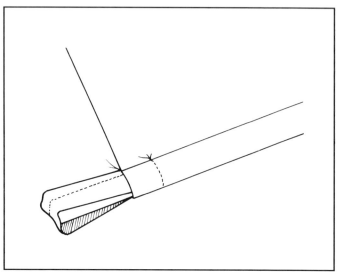

fig 4.11 (h) Elastic pockets. Good for leading edge-spars on deltas and box kite longerons

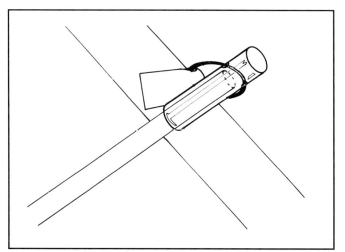

fig 4.11 (f) Tube and ring: widely used on a range of designs and particularly good with polythene kites. Except where otherwise described, this method of spar connection has been used to construct almost all the kites featured in later chapters

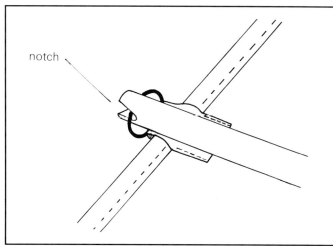

fig 4.11 (i) Notch and ring. Used as spreader bar connection, particularly on large deltas.

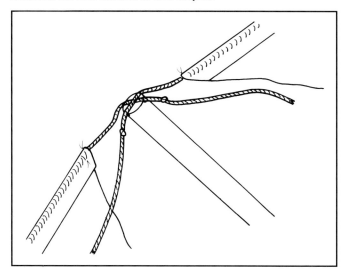

fig 4.11 (g) Another variation of 4.11 (a). Here used to secure the cross spar to two wings of a multi-winged box kite.

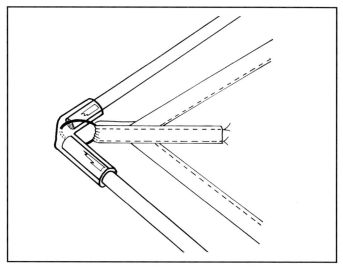

fig 4.11 (j) Standard form of corner connection used on almost all externally-braced kites, made by threading a small split ring through a hole in a length of PVC tube.

▲ Peter Lynn box kites

▼ Six wing corner kite (Tyvek)

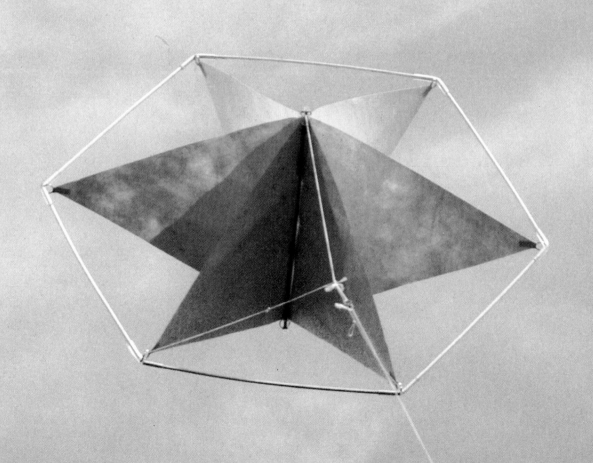

▲ Parafoil I

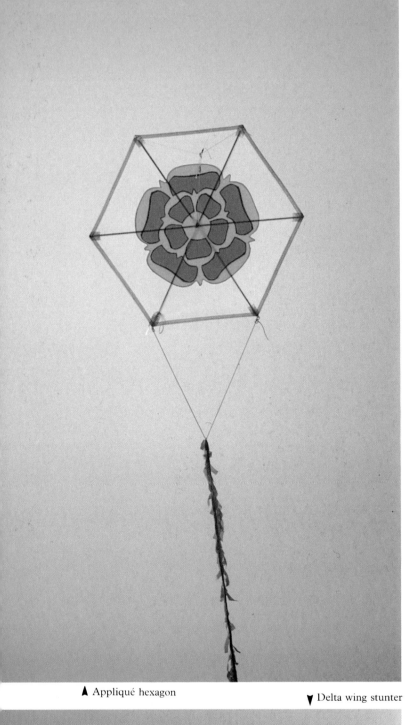

▲ Appliqué hexagon

▼ Delta wing stunter

▲ Folded keel delta

▼ Sputnik

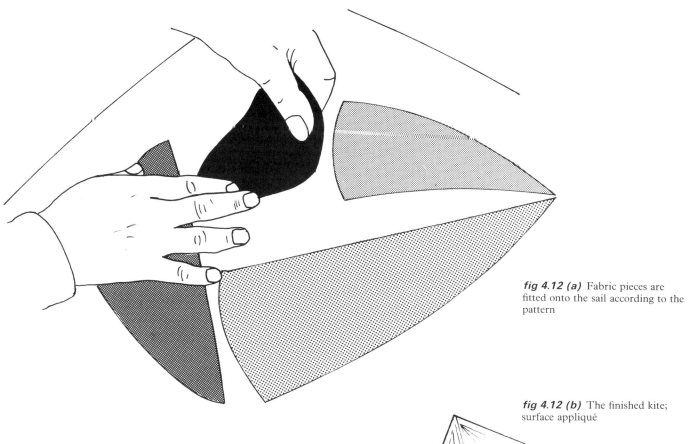

fig 4.12 (a) Fabric pieces are fitted onto the sail according to the pattern

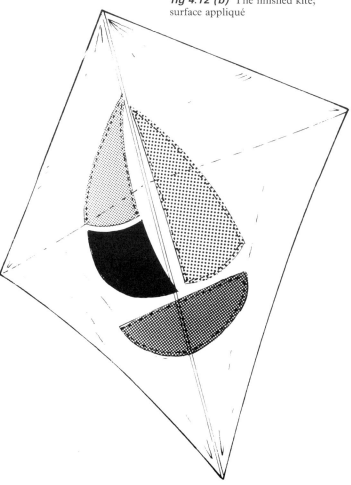

fig 4.12 (b) The finished kite; surface appliqué

APPLIQUÉ

Appliqué is a method of creating intricate designs on your kite, usually reserved for the more experienced kitemakers – not that this should deter the novice from trying. There are essentially two techniques, surface appliqué and cut-away appliqué. Whichever you choose, it is imperative that your design is planned meticulously.

Surface appliqué

This is the simplest technique, used not only on kites but also on other articles such as quilts and garments. It can also be used with paper and polythene.

Draw your design on a large sheet of paper and cut out the shapes. Using these as templates, cut out pieces of fabric, making allowances for overlaps of about 3 mm ($\frac{1}{8}$ inch) at the junction of any two colours. Fit and sew the individual pieces into place on the sail with a narrow straight or zig-zag stitch (Fig 4.12).

With this method of appliqué the background colour is usually the lightest of the range used.

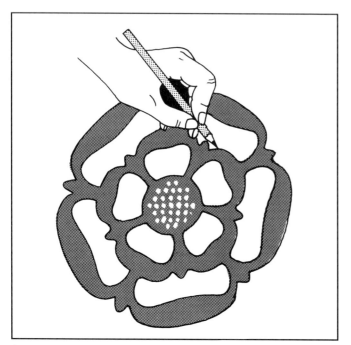

fig 4.13 Draw the design on the front of the fabric.

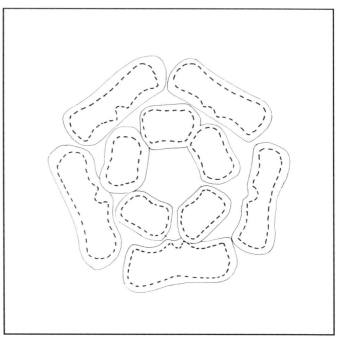

fig 4.14 Turn the fabric over, to fit the coloured patches in place. Sew them in position along the lines previously drawn

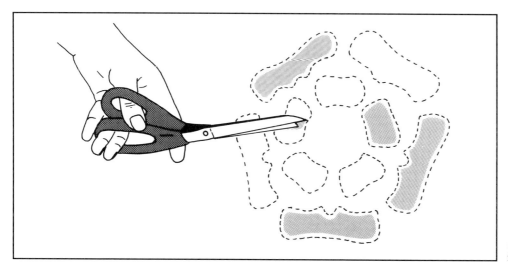

fig 4.15 Cut away the background fabric to reveal the inserted colours

Cut-away appliqué

When designing kite appliqué the aim is to try and create the effect of a stained-glass window, highlighting the pattern as the sun shines through. With cut-away appliqué this effect is enhanced if the background colour is the darkest of the range used.

Again I prefer to use a template and find that it not only helps in creating the design, but also with matching the pieces and balancing the colours.

Draw the design on to a light piece of card with a clear separation of 6 mm ($\frac{1}{4}$ inch) between any two intended colours (Fig 4.13). Tape or lightly glue (aerosol) the piece of rip-stop in the outline colour to a flat board face up and mark out the design using the template.

From your scrap box select the colours required and cut out the shapes using the template. Do however remember to allow a large initial overlap. Turn the sail fabric over and

lightly glue (aerosol) or pin each piece into position, face down (Fig 4.14). Now sew each piece along the lines previously drawn, and when all the pieces are in position cut away the background fabric to reveal the inserted colours (Fig 4.15).

Because spinnaker stretches by only a limited amount, retaining the direction of the weave in both the background colour and inserted pieces is important although not absolutely critical, especially where the design is small in relation to the size of the sail. With softer, more stretchy fabrics the difference in weave direction becomes important, and if the final kite is to fly as well as look attractive, it is imperative that you maintain the integrity of the weave throughout.

One final point with appliqué. It is probably easier to create the design first on a larger sheet of fabric and cut out the sail shape afterwards than to try to do it the other way round.

SPARS

Cutting and trimming

Dowel may be cut with hacksaw or craft knife, rolling it under the blade (Fig 4.16). Fibreglass, on the other hand, must be sawn. In either case it is a good practice to trim or smooth the spar end to ensure a neater fit into the pockets, and of course to reduce wear.

Joints

Inevitably designs will require spars to be joined, either to facilitate easy transport or as a feature of the design. Two types of joint are consequently required, flexible and rigid.

Rigid joints

Rigid joints, to connect a spar along its length, for example, can be made of aluminium alloy, brass or possibly polycarbonate tube in a single butt joint (Fig 4.17).

Four-way joints utilising a central hinge pin can be made from similar materials (Fig 4.18) but it is not possible to create a three-way or flat four-way joint in this way without welding.

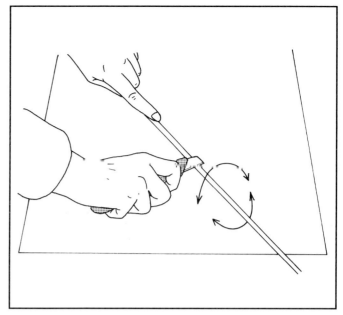

fig 4.16 Standard method of cutting wooden spars

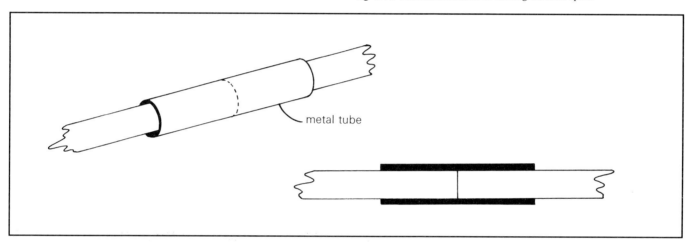

fig 4.17 A 180° rigid joint made from metal tube

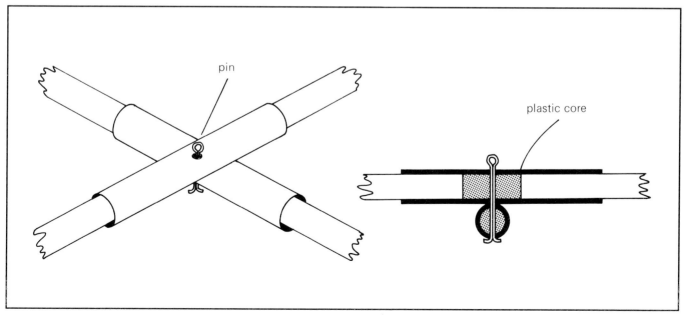

fig 4.18 A 4-way hinged joint made from metal tube

Dihedrals

Dihedrals can be made from metal tubes by bending to the required angle and fitting, as in Fig 4.19. This method is generally used where the vertical and horizontal spars cannot be joined directly in the same plane – the Flare, for example.

Where both spars can be joined it is much easier to buy moulded dihedrals, which may be obtained in a range of sizes from kite stores at nominal cost.

Flexible joints

Where the design of the kite calls for a flexible joint, or where absolute rigidity is not necessary, then joints can be easily made from PVC tube. Fig 4.20 (a)–(f) illustrate a range of possible joints.

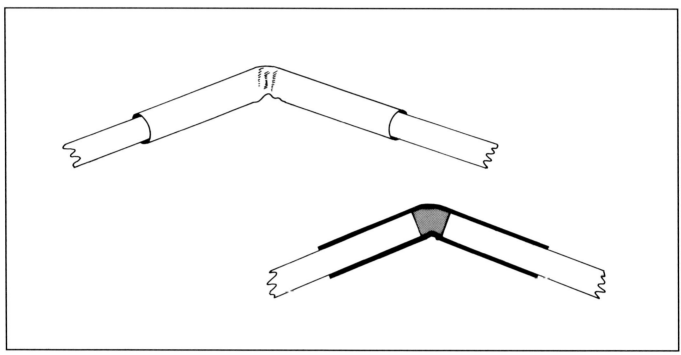

fig 4.19 Dihedral junction made by carefully bending a short length of metal tube

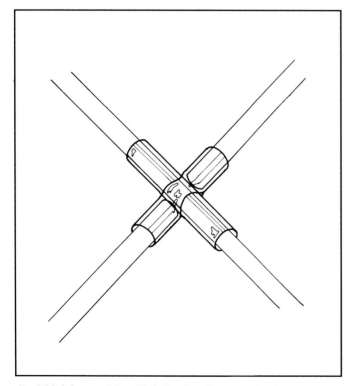

fig 4.20 (a) 4-way joint. Made by threading one tube through a hole in the other

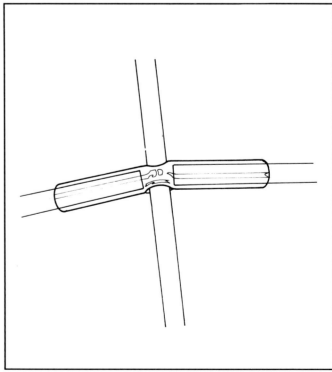

fig 4.20 (b) Similar to 4.20 (a)

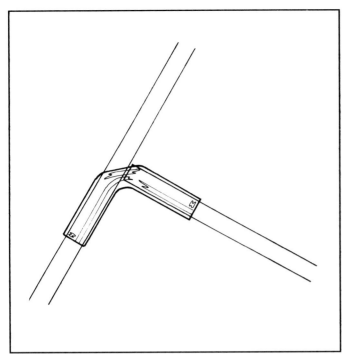

fig 4.20 (c) Right-angle joint

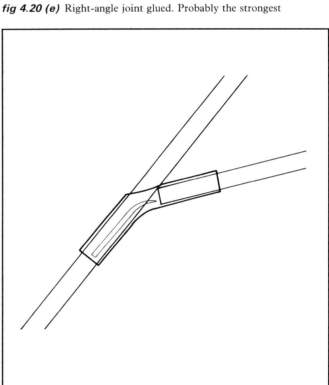

fig 4.20 (e) Right-angle joint glued. Probably the strongest

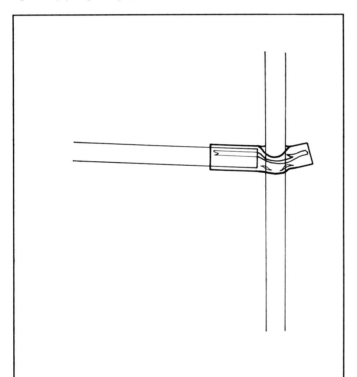

fig 4.20 (d) Similar right-angle joint

fig 4.20 (f) Multi-angle joint

KNOTS

The use or misuse of particular knots in kite construction is one of those hoary subjects which raises its head from time to time and kite literature is full of examples of knots together with pages of calculations all proving or disproving the advantages of one over the other.

My own approach to knots is simple; learn about half a dozen, but be able to tie them behind your back, standing on one leg and in a force 6 wind – well enough so that you don't have to think about it. A minimum range of knots is illustrated in Fig 4.21 (a)–(f).

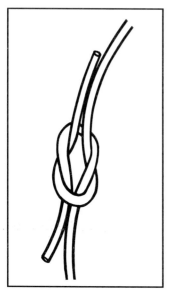

fig 4.21 (a) Reef knot

fig 4.21 (b) Tiller hitch

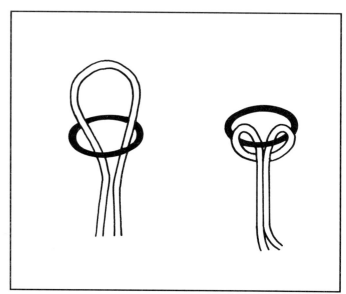

fig 4.21 (e) Lark's head hitch; used extensively to secure the towing ring to the bridle

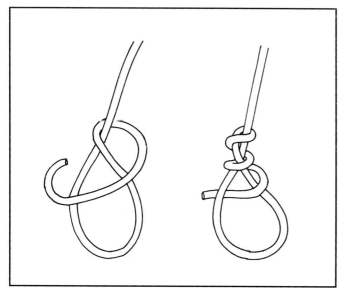

fig 4.21 (c) Blood knot

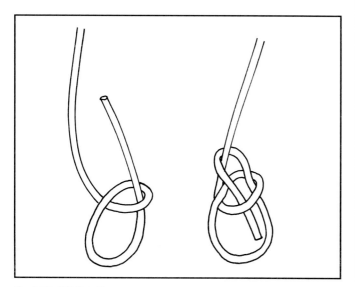

fig 4.21 (d) Bowline

fig 4.21 (f) Knot used to store large number of bridles or shrouds

CHAPTER FIVE

go fly your kite

When I first started making kites, I was always so excited by my latest creation that I wanted to fly it immediately, whatever the weather conditions: storm, rain or calm. It was only after a number of crashes, broken spars and ripped sails that I began to realise that this really just wasn't the way to enjoy kitemaking. So, however impatient you may be to see your newly constructed kite high amongst the clouds, the inevitable disaster and disappointment can be avoided by taking a few minutes to think!

Firstly, remember that your kite has been designed to fly in a fairly limited range of wind speeds, usually between 5 and 15 mph. In very calm conditions it may not fly at all, however much you may run and tug at the line. If, on the other hand, the wind is too strong, it will not only mar the kite's performance, sending it dashing all over the sky, but may also cause some permanent damage – break the spars or stretch the sail fabric, for example. So before you rush out in an attempt to fly your new kite, try to assess the wind conditions. Table 5.1 illustrates signs to look for.

A kite which is easy to assemble at home may not be so in an open field with the wind pulling on the sails. It is a good idea, therefore, to learn to assemble, disassemble and adjust it out of the wind, in your garden or garage perhaps. Try this several times, and each time the process will come easier, such that out on the field it can be achieved without difficulty.

Because kites are generally regarded as children's toys it is easy to be misled into thinking they are completely safe. In responsible hands, yes, kites are safe, but they can also be very dangerous, capable of causing considerable damage and injury. So be very careful!

Although much kite safety is common sense, a simple code has been devised just to remind you.

Table 5.1

Wind strength

Beaufort Scale	Wind speed (mph)	Description	Visible signs
0	1	Calm	Smoke rises
1	2	Light	Smoke drifts
2	5	Light Breeze	Leaves rustle
3	10	Gentle Breeze	Leaves move Lighter branches sway
4	15	Moderate Breeze	Branches move
5	20	Fresh Breeze	Small trees sway
6	25	Strong Breeze	Larger branches move

It is not advisable to fly any sort of kite in above Force 6 winds.

Where to fly – Choose a safe place away from people, property, roads and trees. Keep especially clear of telephone and overhead power cables.

– Do not fly anywhere in the vicinity (within 5 km, 3 miles) of an airfield.

Line – Use the line recommended for the kite. If in doubt use the formula suggested in chapter 3.

– Do not allow your kite to fly above the safe or legal limit. In Britain this is 60 metres (200 feet).

Wind – Fly the kite only in the wind conditions specified. Flying in too strong a wind will not only make the kite difficult to control but will also cause permanent damage.

Gloves – Always wear gloves when flying a kite, however small. Even light kite-line can cause very painful burns and cuts.

CHOOSING THE CORRECT PLACE TO FLY

Choosing a good place to fly your kite is not only a matter of safety, but one of the skills experienced kitefliers develop.

Winds at ground level are greatly influenced by terrain, constantly changing their speed and direction. Obstacles such as buildings or trees will create currents which may affect the performance of your kite. At best it will be a bit skittish and difficult to launch, but if you're not too careful these currents will toss the kite over the sky, making it impossible to control, and of course spoil your enjoyment (Fig 5.1 (a)).

Wind speed also increases with height, which leads many people to believe that the best place to fly a kite is on the top of a hill. This is one of those myths which, although not wholly wrong, is not totally right either. Kites do fly well on hills, but only on one side – the windward side. Flying a kite on the leeward side, where it is jostled around in the turbulence, is just asking for trouble (Fig 5.1 (b)).

The best places to fly a kite are open fields, beaches or moorland where there are no obstacles to disturb the air currents. If you must fly near buildings or on hills, ensure that you are on the windward side (Fig 5.2 (a), (b)).

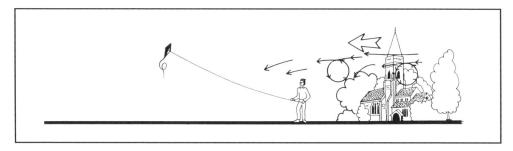

fig 5.1 (a) Obstacles such as buildings or trees can cause currents which may affect the performance of your kite

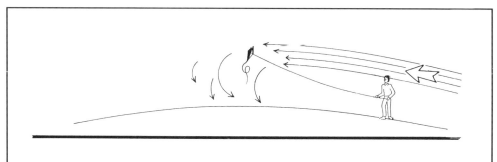

fig 5.1 (b) Flying on hills is fine, but do be clear to fly on the windward side. On the leeward side the kite is likely to be tossed about in the turbulence

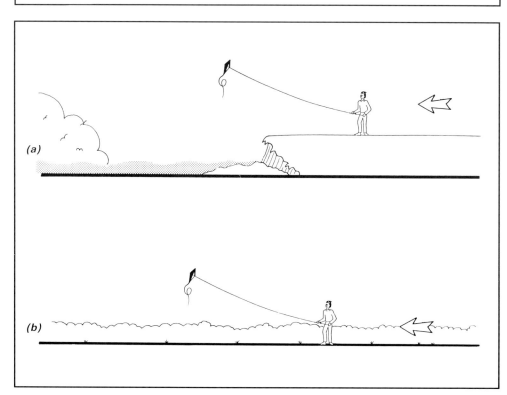

fig 5.2 The best places to fly kites are (a) beaches or (b) open moorland free from obstacles

LAUNCH AND LANDING

Beginners often find launching a kite very difficult, but if you're patient enough to learn, it does become easier and like the experts you will be able to just toss the kite into the air to see it rise perfectly. What you should never do, however, is run with the kite dragging behind your back: this achieves little.

Part of the skill of a good launch is learning how to set the bridle correctly. Generally speaking, in stronger winds you should set the kite to fly at a lower angle of attack by sliding the towing ring along the bridle just a *little* way towards the tip of the kite. In lighter winds, to generate sufficient lift a much higher angle of attack might be required. To do this, slide the towing ring along the bridle towards the base (Fig 5.3). Kites react differently to such changes, particularly in their stability, and much can only be learned by experiment.

Assisted launch

This is usually used by beginners, or on kites which are a little skittish in ground turbulence.

Tie the line to the towing point and unwind about 5–6 metres (16–20 feet) of line. Lightly take hold of the line in your stronger hand, reel in the other, and ask your helper to stand facing the wind with the kite held upright in front of them. When you feel a gust of wind, signal your helper to let go of the kite. As it begins to rise, gradually pay out the line (Fig 5.4).

Single-handed launch

This is the more expert approach. Tie the line to the towing point and unwind about 4–5 metres (13–16 feet). Hold the line and reel in your stronger hand, the kite in the other. When you feel a gust, drop the kite into the wind tugging gently on the line. As the kite begins to rise, gradually pay out the line (Fig 5.5).

Winch launch

The winch launch is usually a second stage of the first two launches.

You may find that as you pay out the line, it starts to go slack and the kite starts to fall, possibly twisting out of the wind as it does so. If this happens give the line a good tug, and as the kite rises slowly pay out further line, trying to maintain tension (Fig 5.6). You may have to do this several times to lift the kite into the upper air currents.

High-start launch

In very light ground winds, when none of the previous launches works, then a high-start launch is the only option left. It is also the only occasion when you might need to run with your kite, and even then only as an absolute last resort.

With the line tied to the towing point, set the kite in position, or ask someone to hold it 15–20 metres (50–60 feet) down wind. With both hands on the reel tension the line and give it a sustained tug, lifting the kite into the wind. If you have to run at this stage, do so steadily, keeping control of the line, and remain facing the kite as much as you can. As the kite lifts into stronger air currents, continue with the winch launch (Fig 5.7).

Landing

Landing a kite is sometimes more difficult than launching. Your aim is of course to bring it back to the ground, but at the same time you should also try to maintain control of its descent, ensuring that you neither damage the kite, nor cause danger to people or property around you.

If the line is relatively slack, it may be possible to bring the kite in directly. Wind the line slowly and carefully by hand around the reel or handle keeping control of both the line and the kite (Fig 5.8).

In much stronger conditions, where you are unable to effectively control the kite with one hand, the only option is to peg the line to the ground and haul the kite down arm over arm. A volunteer to assist with winding the line is very useful here. Never be tempted to wind the kite down directly on to the reel, for as you do so the tension of the line already on the reel will increase several-fold. Although not causing it to break, this will severely weaken it.

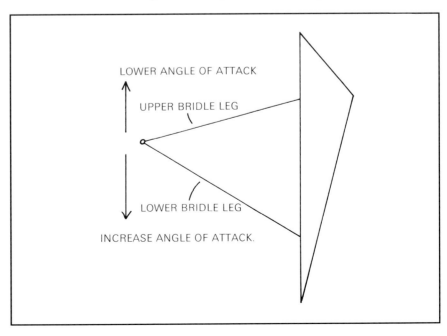

fig 5.3 Part of the skill of a successful launch is setting the towing point correctly

fig 5.4 Assisted launch

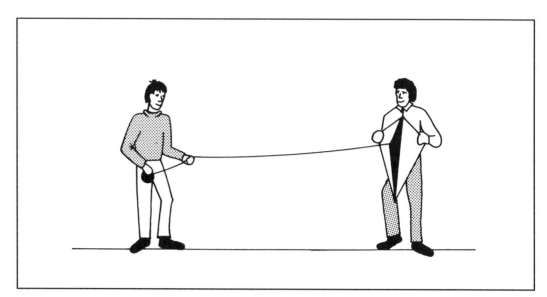

fig 5.5 Single-handed launch

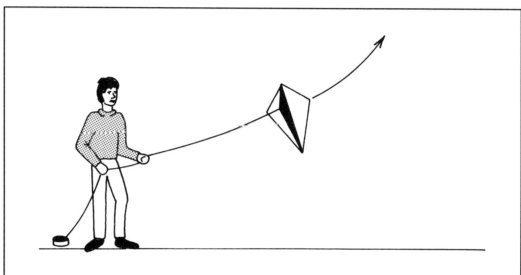

fig 5.6 Winch launch

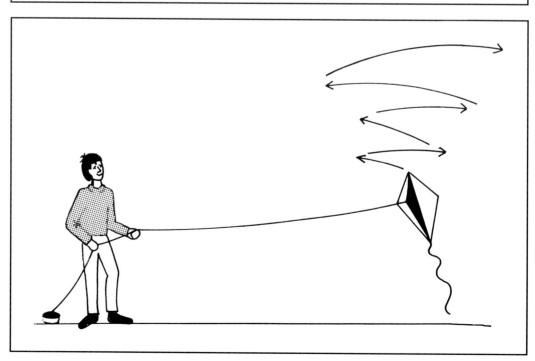

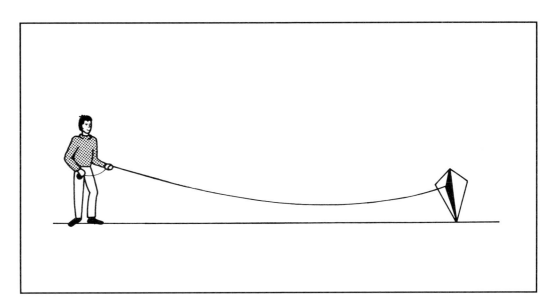

fig 5.7 High-start launch

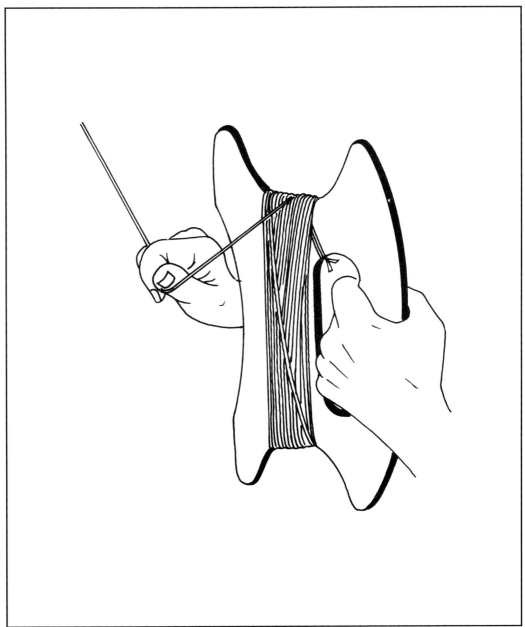

fig 5.8 Wind the line carefully by hand around the handle

WHAT TO DO WHEN THINGS GO WRONG

By the time most commercially-made kites reach the shops they have undergone fairly rigorous testing in a wide range of conditions, but in time the fabric will stretch, and spars may have to be replaced or bridles/shrouds refitted. All of these can affect flying characteristics and some trimming will be necessary. Home-made kites also suffer from the inexperience of the maker and certainly maiden flights are often less than successful.

Symptom	Possible cause/correction
Line is slack, the kite will not rise	– Lower the towing point
	– Wind insufficient; try again another day
Line is tight, the kite will not rise	– Lift the towing point
	– Wind is too strong; try again another day
	– Design/construction fault; kite too heavy; poor lift/drag ratio
On launch kite tips over	– Design/construction fault
	– Too high centre of gravity – replace upper spars with ones of lower weight
	– Add a high drag/heavy tail
	– Add a weight to base (if nothing else works!)
As line is pulled kite tips forward	– Lower the towing point
	– Severely bent spine/longeron: replace it
Kite pulls to one side	– Construction fault caused by imbalance of tension/weight in opposite sides of the sail. Hold the kite by the towing point and check balance
	– Uneven bridle legs: check these
	– Misaligned keel or tail
Kite is slow to recover from sideways gust (oscillating – yaw)	– Design/construction fault. Too low a centre of gravity
	– Add a high drag tail
	– Lower the towing point
Kite sluggish, slow to recover from sideways gust (wandering)	– Design/construction fault
	– Reduce dihedral
	– Add a weight to the base (if you really must!)
	– Add a heavy tail

Symptom	Possible cause/correction
In an increasing wind kite tips to one side making a large circle as it falls	– Imbalance of sails; one side possibly stretched
	– Loose sails flapping to one side of the kite
	– Mis-aligned keel, check it
	– Increase dihedral
Line pulls tight. Kite oscillates rapidly from side to side (roll)	– Kite is flying at too high an angle of attack. Lift the towing point
	– Wind conditions too strong. Try again another day
	– Lengthen bridle
Kite oscillates back and forth (pitching)	– Possible design fault. Kite too heavy or centre of gravity too low
	– Horizontal spars too weak and are bending. Lift the towing point
	– Increase the length of the bridle

plane surface kites

Plane surface kites are, of course, the oldest and most widely flown. In this section I have tried to include some of the modern classics together with some pretty unusual innovations.

FLYING SAUCER (*Soucoupe Volante*)

The most interesting kite I have come across in some time and based on a design by Jacques Zanni published in *Le Lucane*, the French Kite Society newsletter.

Sail	: 6 mm (¼ inch) expanded polystyrene
Spars	: None
Line	: 2–3 kg (5–7 lb)
Tail	: None
Wind speed	: Gentle – fresh
Time to make	: 1–3 hrs
Difficulty	: ★★

fig 6.1

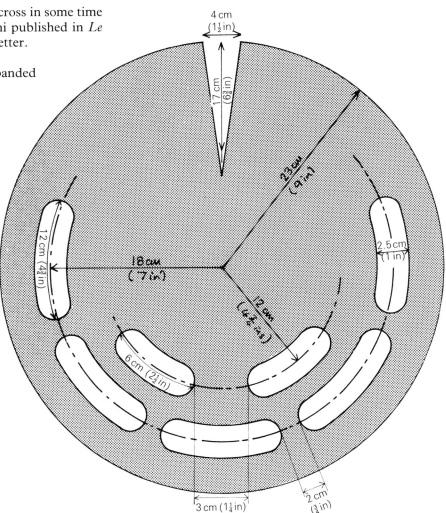

Cut out the sail and fins according to the patterns (Fig 6.1, 6.2).

You may find it useful to bevel the edges where the top slice of the circle has been removed, as this will facilitate an easier join.

Glue the edges of this top slice to create the convex saucer shape, but as this will create just a little tension it is probably better to leave the adhesive to set, perhaps overnight.

Glue the fins as indicated (Fig 6.3). A slight improvement in performance is achieved if the fins and leading edge of the saucer are streamlined. Do this with a knife and sandpaper, probably easier after they have been fixed in place. Punch and reinforce holes for the bridle. Fit a two-leg 1 m (3 feet) bridle to the points indicated.

Although this version of the saucer is extremely stable over a wide range of wind speeds, its flying angle is relatively low, about 70 degrees.

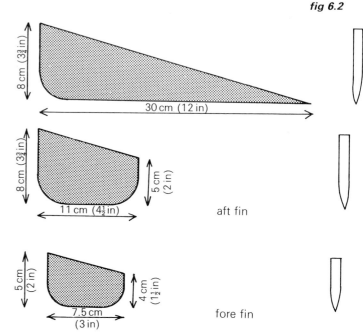

fig 6.2

8 cm (3¾ in)

30 cm (12 in)

8 cm (3¾ in)

11 cm (4½ in)

5 cm (2 in)

aft fin

5 cm (2 in)

7.5 cm (3 in)

4 cm (1½ in)

fore fin

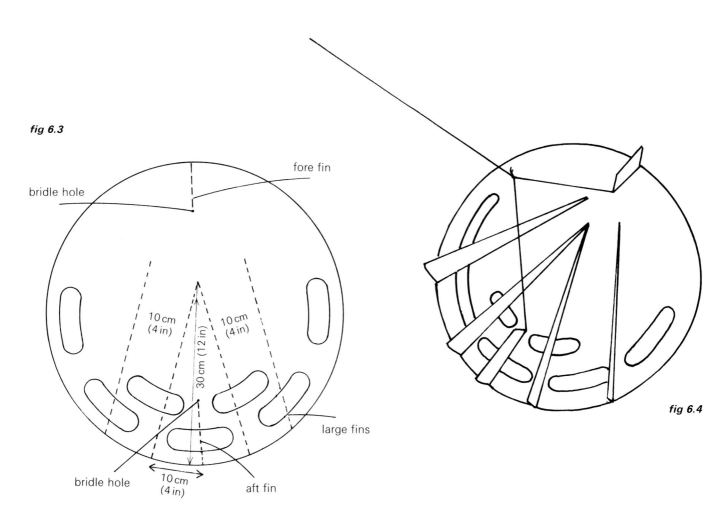

fig 6.3

bridle hole

fore fin

10 cm (4 in)   10 cm (4 in)

30 cm (12 in)

large fins

bridle hole

10 cm (4 in)

aft fin

fig 6.4

WHITE DOVE

Another interesting expanded polystyrene kite rather loosely based on a design by John Spendlove published in the Belgian Magazine *Le Journal de Nouveau Cervoliste Belge*. John has an annoying habit of giving his kites codes rather than names, this one he calls XPB (Xpanded Polystyrene Bird – Ugh!).

Sail	: 2 mm ($\frac{1}{8}$ inch) expanded polystyrene
Spars	: Ribs made from 6 mm ($\frac{1}{4}$ inch) polystyrene strips
Line	: 2–3 kg (5–7 lb)
Tail	: None
Wind speeds	: Light
Time to make	: 1–2 hrs
Difficulty	: ★★

Cut out the main wing shape as one piece from a sheet of 2 mm ($\frac{1}{8}$ inch) polystyrene, then the body shape and ribs from 6 mm ($\frac{1}{4}$ inch) (Fig 6.5). Glue the body to the wings, then fit the ribs in place on the rear surface. Both the wings and tail should end up with a dihedral angle of about 165 degrees (Fig 6.6).

Fix an 80 cm (32 inch) bridle to the points indicated.

The Dove prefers light steady conditions, but will take quite a bit of buffeting before it needs an additional tail.

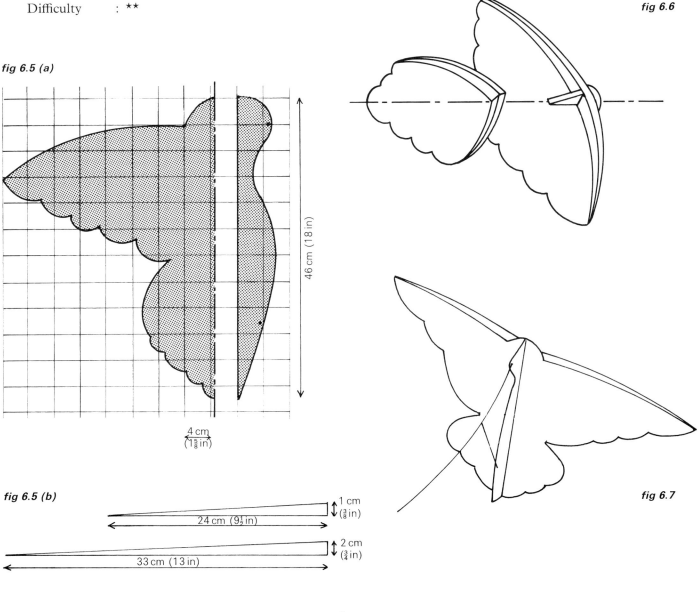

fig 6.5 (a)

46 cm (18 in)

4 cm ($1\frac{5}{8}$ in)

fig 6.5 (b)

1 cm ($\frac{3}{8}$ in)

24 cm ($9\frac{1}{2}$ in)

2 cm ($\frac{3}{4}$ in)

33 cm (13 in)

2 cm ($\frac{3}{4}$ in)

5 cm (2 in)

fig 6.6

fig 6.7

PEARSON ROLLER

A very popular design based on Alick Pearson's original.

Sail	: Rip-stop nylon
Spars	: Ramin dowel 8 mm ($\frac{5}{16}$ inch). Spine 122 cm (48 inches) Spars; upper 2 pieces 58.5 cm (23 inches); lower 2 pieces 61 cm (24 inches)
Additional materials	: 20–35 SWG aluminium tube of 8 mm ($\frac{5}{16}$ inch) internal diameter or equivalent brass
Line	: 35 kg (75 lb)
Tail	: Tailless
Wind speeds	: Light–gentle
Time to make	: 4–6 hrs
Difficulty	: ★★★

Make templates according to the pattern (Fig 6.8), adding allowances for hemming, although a 12 mm ($\frac{1}{2}$ inch) tape binding is recommended. Place the marked centre line along the fold in the fabric and cut out the sails as single pieces.

Cut out the rudder, making a double hem on three sides, and sew a 12 mm ($\frac{1}{2}$ inch) tape along the diagonal to allow a short dowel batten to be fitted.

Sew the rudder to the lower sail along the centre axis. Make and fit pockets as indicated (Fig 6.9). The pockets will be subject to a great deal of stress and should be strong, made from a double fold of fabric and well stitched. The two sails are connected via a wide tape 10 cm (4 inches) long, although it may be preferable to extend the tape along the whole length of the kite, provided of course that the gap between remains 10 cm (4 inches).

Sew ties, 12 mm ($\frac{1}{2}$ inch) binding tape, 45 cm (8 inches) long, to the mid-points of the sails as indicated and a small tape loop to the tip of the rudder. Fit eyelets at the wing tips and join the sails with bracing lines as indicated.

The dihedrals are made from 8 mm ($\frac{5}{16}$ inch) diameter alloy/brass tube, 15 cm (6 inches) long, bent to form an angle of 150 degrees. You will need two of these.

Unlike many other designs, the sail on the Roller is set extremely tight. First fit and trim the spine so that it tensions the sail, and tie it in place. Then fit and trim the spars, again tensioning the sail sufficiently to give the spine a slight forward camber. Tie the spars in place. Make and reinforce two holes in the upper sail at the dihedral to accept the 4-metre (13 feet) bridle and connect the other end to the rudder tip.

On their maiden flight Rollers are apt to pull to one side, and some trimming may be necessary. Do this by adjusting the bracing lines between the sails.

fig 6.8

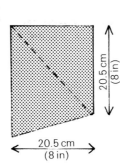

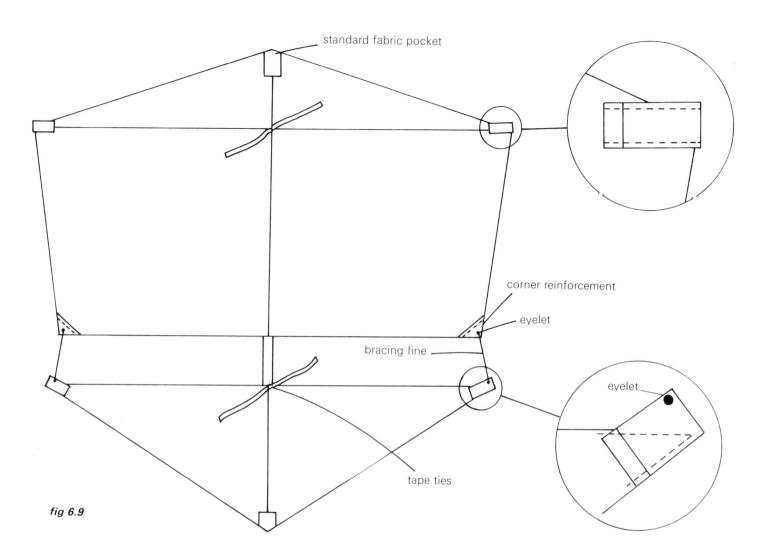

standard fabric pocket

corner reinforcement

eyelet

bracing line

tape ties

eyelet

fig 6.9

fig 6.10

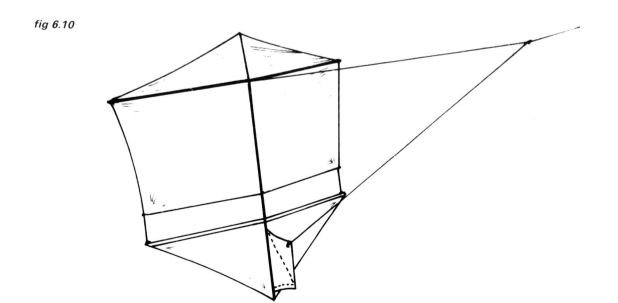

FLARE

A slightly smaller version of David Pelham's original design.

Sail	: Rip-stop nylon
Spars	: Ramin dowel. Longerons 8 mm ($\frac{5}{16}$ inch) 2 pieces 90 cm (36 inches) Spars 8 mm 2 pieces 45 cm (18 inches) and 6.4 mm ($\frac{1}{4}$ inch) × 75 cm (30 inches)
Other materials	: 2 × 15 cm (6 inch) lengths 20–35 SWG aluminium tube of 8 mm ($\frac{5}{16}$ inch) internal diameter, or equivalent brass
Line	: 35 kg (75 lb)
Tail	: Drogue
Wind speeds	: Light–gentle
Time to make	: 4–6 hrs
Difficulty	: ★★★

Cut out the two wings and centre as indicated in Fig 6.11, adding of course allowances for hemming/binding and for the longeron casing. Now cut out two of each fin, similarly hemmed/bound (Fig 6.12).

Using the pattern in Fig 6.13 sew the fins in position, sandwiched between the wing and centrepiece, then the whole is folded in a sort of French seam to create a central casing for the longerons, similar to the construction of fabric deltas (Fig 6.14). Don't forget to include 30 cm (12 inch) tape ties for both upper and lower spars. Reinforce the longeron casing at the top and bottom with a small square of fabric, again using the technique described for fabric deltas.

Now make pockets at the corners as indicated and fit tape loops at the tips of the fins (Fig 6.15). Cut two dihedrals from 8 mm ($\frac{5}{16}$ inch) internal brass or aluminium tube bent to an angle of 165 degrees. Fit the longerons tight into the casings.

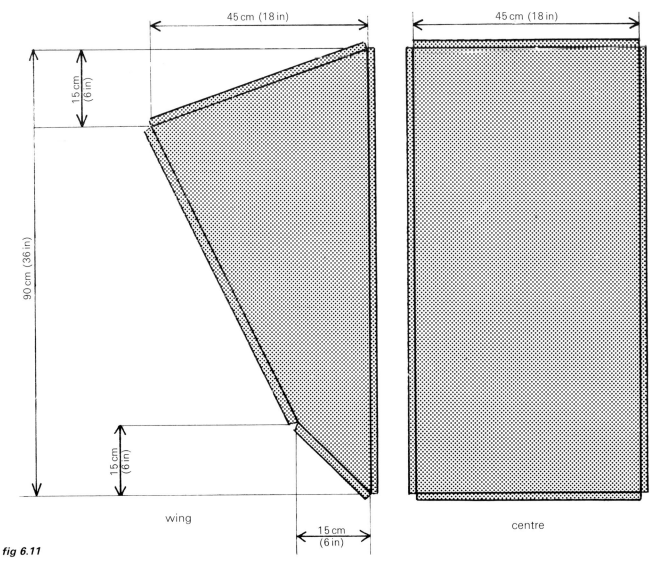

45 cm (18 in) 45 cm (18 in)

15 cm (6 in)

90 cm (36 in)

15 cm (6 in)

wing

15 cm (6 in)

centre

fig 6.11

The upper spars 8 mm ($\frac{5}{16}$ inch) diameter are also fitted tight, tensioning the sail to give the longerons a slight forward camber. Tie the dihedrals in position.

The lower spar, 6.4 mm ($\frac{1}{4}$ inch) Ramin, is also fitted tight to bow. Tie this in position.

The Flare has a four-leg bridle consisting of two 4 m (13 feet) loops tied one to the upper and one to the lower fin. These bridles are then joined to each other at their centres via a third piece of short line, to which the towing ring is attached, allowing fine adjustments to be made easily.

Although this version of the Flare is reasonably stable in light, steady winds it will of course require a drogue in more turbulent conditions.

Reproduced with acknowledgement to David Pelham, *Penguin Book of Kites*.

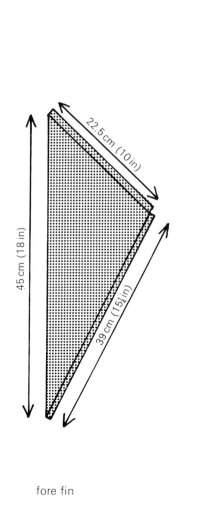

fore fin

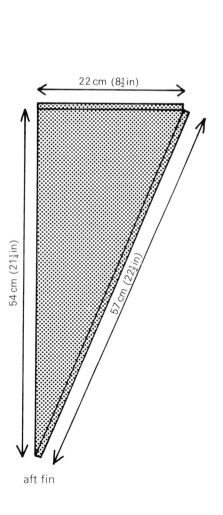

aft fin

fig 6.12

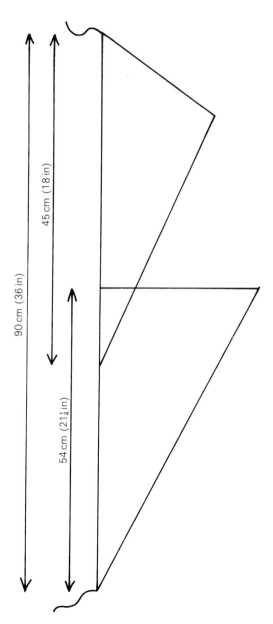

fig 6.13

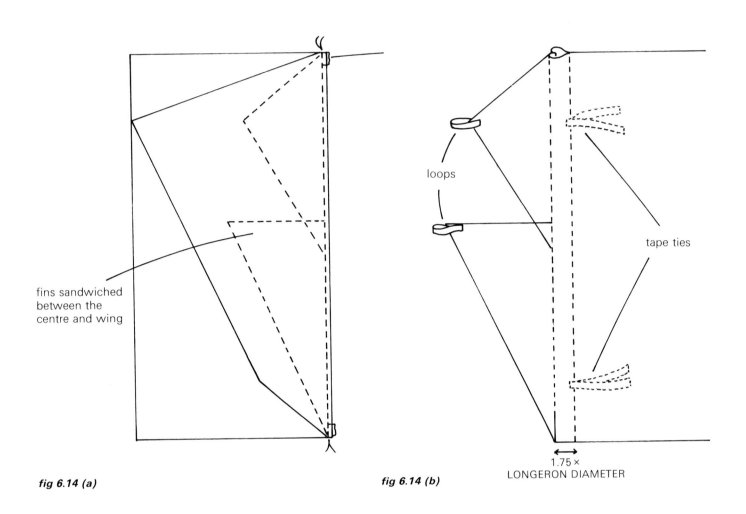

fins sandwiched
between the
centre and wing

fig 6.14 (a)

loops

tape ties

1.75 ×
LONGERON DIAMETER

fig 6.14 (b)

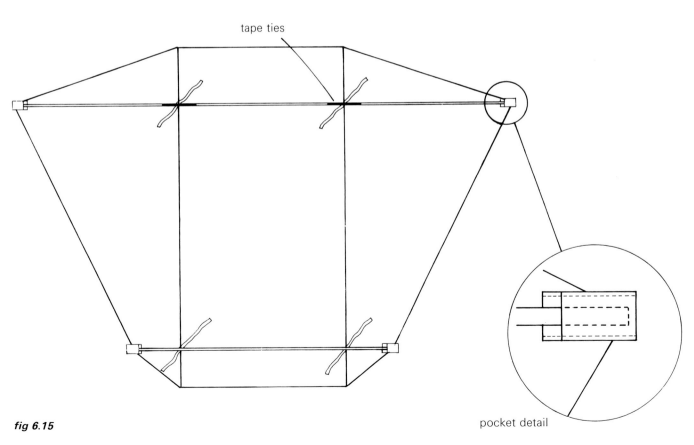

tape ties

fig 6.15

pocket detail

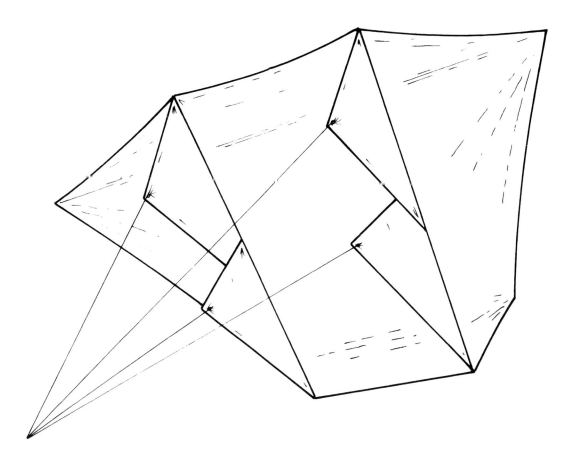

fig 6.16

deltas

If it isn't already obvious, my particular passion is for delta kites. Very graceful designs, they're satisfying to make, good for workshops since their construction is quite simple, and ultimately therapeutic to fly.

SPARLESS DELTA

A simplified variation of Francis Rogallo's original Flexikite, this is very easy to make and ideal for workshops with younger children as an alternative to sleds – which are just a little overplayed.

Sail	: Light paper (newspaper?), Mylar, Tyvek, polythene
Spars	: None
Tail	: Flat ribbon, 2–3 metres (6–9 feet)
Line	: 2–3 kg (4–7 lb)
Wind Speed	: Light
Time to make	: 15–30 mins
Difficulty	: ★

Cut your material into a square of 40–60 cm (16–24 inches) sides – exact dimensions do not seem to be critical (Fig 7.1). Reinforce the edges if necessary.

Make a fold along the diagonal and then refold 1 cm (½ inch) either side. Tape or glue a strip of material to the reverse, such that you create a triangular tube of 1 cm (½ inch) side. This will give the spine a little rigidity. If you are using polythene it may instead be necessary to introduce a thin dowel along the spine.

Reinforce points A, B, C and D and punch holes to accept bridles. Fit a four-leg bridle as shown, each leg approximately twice the size of the square used, and add a long 2–3 metres (6–9 feet) lightweight ribbon/crepe paper tail to the bottom corner.

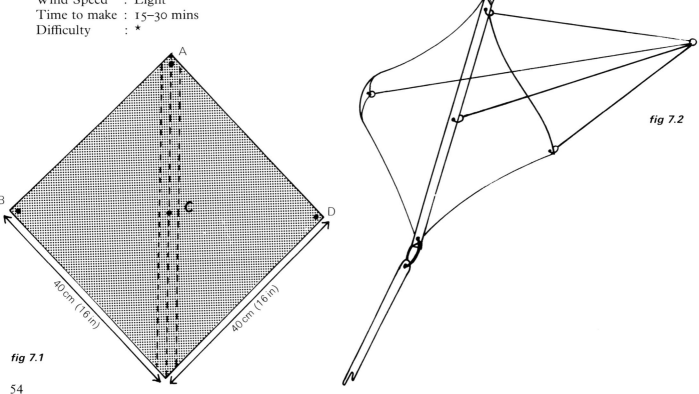

A
B
C
D
40 cm (16 in)
40 cm (16 in)

fig 7.1

fig 7.2

FOLDED KEEL DELTA

Sail : Polythene
Spars : Ramin dowel. Spine 6.4 mm ($\frac{1}{4}$ inch) × 61 cm (24 inches) Leading edge spars 2 pieces 5 mm ($\frac{3}{16}$ inch) × 62 cm (25 inches) Spreader 6.4 mm ($\frac{1}{4}$ inch) × approximately 57 cm (22$\frac{1}{2}$ inches)
Other materials : Small split/'O' ring
Tail : Tailless
Line : 7 kg (15 lb)
Wind speeds : Light–gentle
Time to make : 30 mins–1 hr
Difficulty : ★★

When I first started working on this design I was very surprised by both its lift and stability over a wide range of conditions and my polythene version actually out-performs many of the larger rip-stop deltas.

Fold and crease your sheet of polythene. Place line *AC* of the template along the fold (Fig 7.3), and cut out the sail as one piece. Score a line 1 cm ($\frac{3}{8}$ inch) from the leading edge. Fold and tape it to create spar tubes.

Now mark the line of the keel *AB* on both wings and crease. Then tape the two wings along this line to the rear to create a forward keel (Fig 7.4).

You may find it useful to put 2–3 staples about 1 cm ($\frac{3}{8}$ inch) from the keel edge to hold the spine in position. Fit the spreader bar connections 36 cm (14 inches) from the tip and fit the spine and leading edge spars. Staple the leading edge at the tip end to prevent the spar moving forward.

Fix small pieces of tape at the tip and base of the spine as reinforcement and at the tips of the leading edge. Pay special attention to the spine tip since this point usually has to take the force of most crashes.

Fit a small ring or loop of line, on the spine approximately 34 cm (13$\frac{1}{4}$ inches) from the base. The exact position can only be found by experiment. Tie the line to this ring.

Rip-stop versions of this design also fly particularly well.

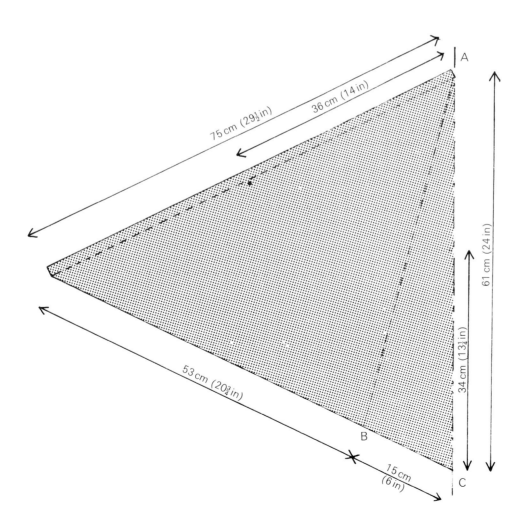

fig 7.3

fig 7.4

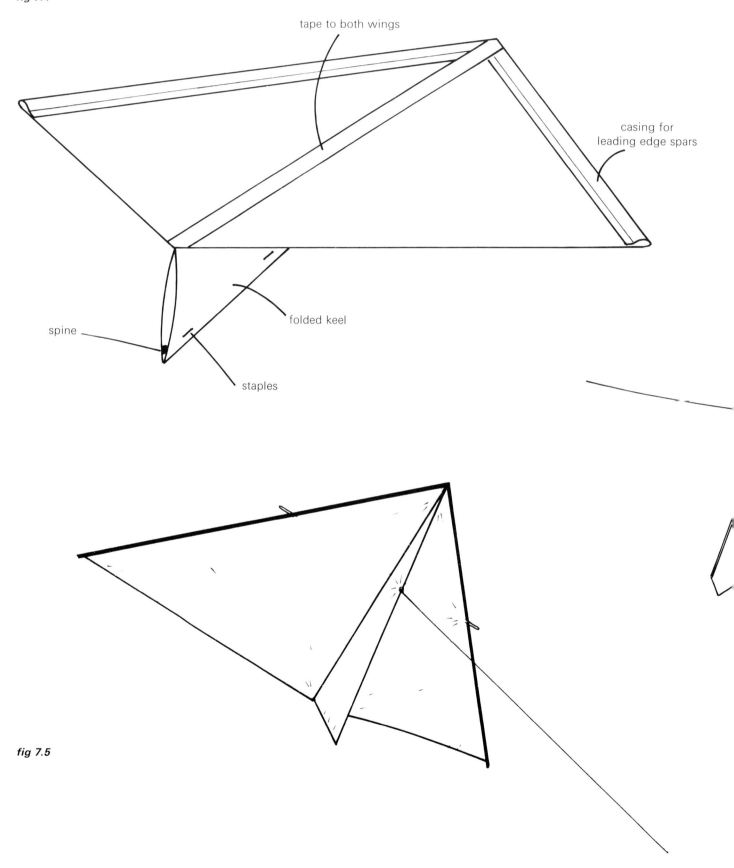

tape to both wings

casing for
leading edge spars

folded keel

spine

staples

fig 7.5

56

SKY DART

Sail	:	Polythene, Tyvek
Spars	:	Ramin dowel. Spine 6.4 mm ($\frac{1}{4}$ inch) × 60 cm (24 inches) Leading edge spars, 2 pieces 5 mm ($\frac{3}{16}$ inch) × 92 cm (36 inches) Spreader bar 6.4 mm ($\frac{1}{4}$ inch) × 58 cm (23 inches)
Other materials	:	Small split or 'O' ring
Tail	:	Tailless
Line	:	7 kg (15 lb)
Wind speed	:	Light–gentle
Time to make	:	30 mins–1 hr
Difficulty	:	★

Cut out two pieces of sail material – one a single wing, the other a wing plus keel – joined along *AB*. On the latter, make a good firm crease along *AB* and join the two pieces with tape along this line (Fig. 7.6).

Score lines 1 cm ($\frac{3}{8}$ inch) from the leading edges, fold and tape to create the spar tubes. Reinforce the edges of the keel with Sellotape or equivalent. Now tape the spine to the rear of the sail, adding some extra reinforcement to the tip since this point will bear the brunt of most crashes.

Make spreader bar connections 36 cm (14 inches) along the leading edge from the tip and fit the leading edge spars. As with the folded keel delta, it is a good idea to staple them in place. Do not connect the line directly to the keel but tape a small ring to the tip. Trim and fit the spreader bar so that the wings sit at a dihedral angle of about 170 degrees (Fig 7.7).

The first time I introduced this kite at a workshop, one bright spark decided he would add a short tail to the wing tips, which the rest of the group duly copied. Now tails are added as standard.

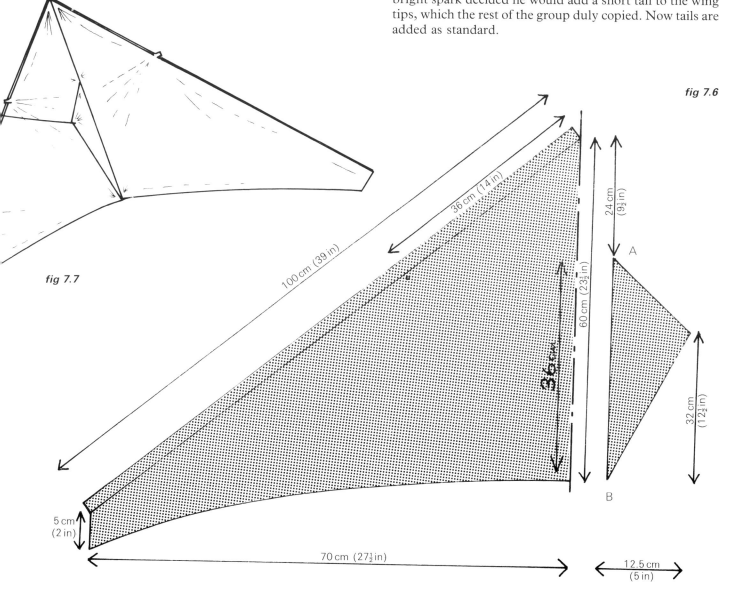

fig 7.6

fig 7.7

ARROWHEAD DELTA

This is one of the deltas I regularly use in workshops. Based on a design by Tony Cartwright, it is not difficult to make and, as Tony himself says, it 'flies at an angle guaranteed to give you neck-ache!'.

I prefer to cut out the Arrowhead as with the Sky Dart, a single wing and a wing plus keel joined along the spine. The rest of the construction is also similar (Fig 7.8).

Sail   : Polythene, Tyvek, newspaper, wrapping paper

Spars   : Ramin dowel. Spine 5 mm ($\frac{3}{16}$ inch) × 58.5 cm (23 inches)
Leading edge spars 2 pieces 5 mm ($\frac{3}{16}$ inch) × 35.5 cm (14 inches)
Spreader 6.4 mm ($\frac{1}{4}$ inch) × 45 cm (18 inches) (approx)

Tail   : Tailless

Line   : 7 kg (15 lb)

Wind speed : Light–gentle

Time to make : 30 mins–1 hr

Difficulty   : ★

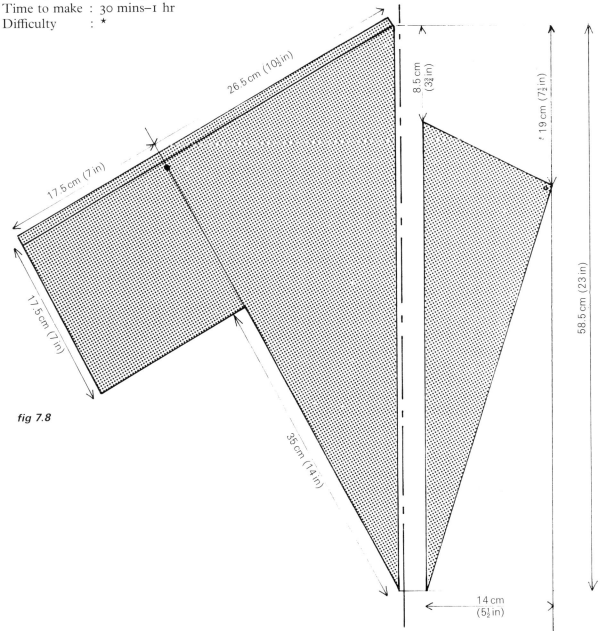

fig 7.8

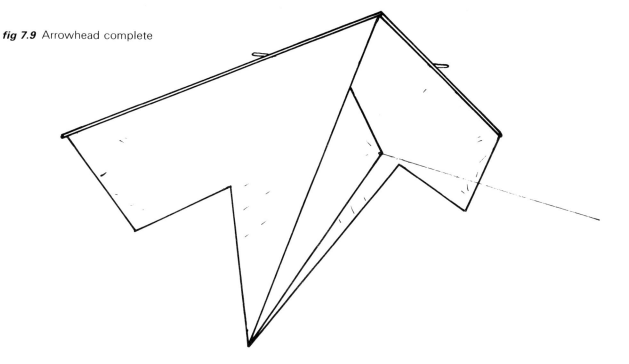

fig 7.9 Arrowhead complete

FABRIC DELTAS

Most of the fabric deltas featured below, although of very different form, share the same basic construction. Rather than repeat details for each design it will be useful to consider first the common features.

The argument as to whether the spine should be placed forward or to the rear of the wings is one which has been raging for some time. Most designers tend to place the spine forward, for no other reason than it means the kite is marginally easier to make. But there is an increasing body of opinion that this method of construction also improves its flying characteristics.

In most cases the wings should be made as two separate pieces, joined along the spine. To create the spine casing lay the wings on top of one another, face to face, ensuring an exact fit, with the keel sandwiched in between (Fig 7.10). Add two small squares of fabric at the tip and base to act as reinforcement and sew a flat seam 3 mm ($\frac{1}{8}$ inch) from the edge. Fold the wings back on themselves, and using a domestic iron press along the seam. Make a second seam 1.75 times the diameter of the spine from the edge, to create the casing.

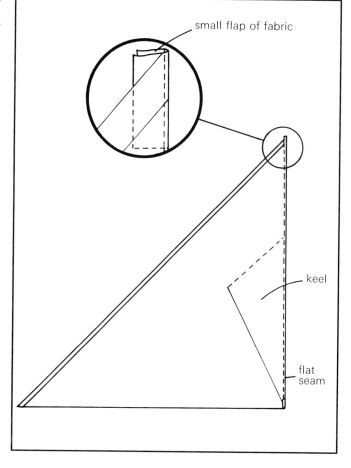

small flap of fabric

keel

flat seam

fig 7.10

Do not sew right up to the trailing edge but stop a distance 1.75 times the diameter of the spine from the end, and reinforce by backstitching. This will assist the insertion and removal of the spine. Stitch across the ends of the casing (Fig 7.11).

Casing for the leading edge spars is also made quite simply. Fold and make a hem 5 mm ($\frac{3}{16}$ inch) deep. Fold the fabric again to a depth of 1.75 times the diameter of the spar and sew again. Make a break in the stitching as shown. This will facilitate easy insertion and withdrawal of the spar. Reinforce the wing tip with an additional layer of fabric (Fig 7.12).

Spreader bar connections are more a matter of choice. I tend to use a tube and ring on a tape loop or notched spreader. A number of methods is illustrated in Chapter 5.

Except where otherwise stated, the spine is usually fitted tight, as are the leading edge spars, so that there is a slight puckering of the fabric. The spreader bar is similarly fitted snug, but not so tight that the sail surface becomes distorted.

Flying line may be connected to the keel by tape loops set 2 cm ($\frac{3}{4}$ inch) apart, or alternatively by the insertion of eyelets at the tip of the keel. In either case, however, the keel tip should be reinforced with an additional layer of fabric (Fig 7.13).

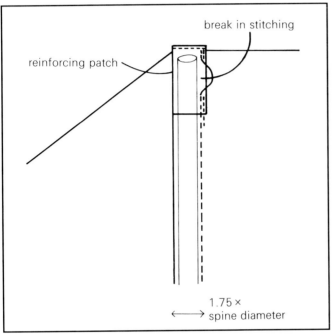

fig 7.11

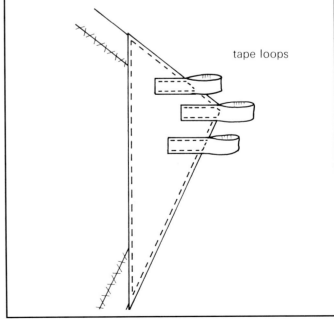

fig 7.13 (a)

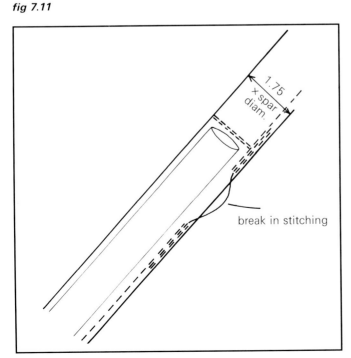

fig 7.12

fig 7.13 (b)

OPEN KEEL DELTA

Based on Ed Grauel's widely published design.

Sail	:	Rip-stop nylon
Spars	:	Ramin dowel. Spine 6.4 mm ($\frac{1}{4}$ inch) × 86.5 cm (34 inches) Leading edge spars 2 pieces 6.4 mm ($\frac{1}{4}$ inch) × 71 cm (28 inches) Spreader 6.4 mm ($\frac{1}{4}$ inch) × 90 cm (36 inches) (approx)
Tail	:	Tailless
Line	:	15 kg (35 lb)
Wind speeds	:	Light–gentle
Time to make	:	2–4 hrs
Difficulty	:	★★★

Make templates as indicated in Fig 7.14. Both the keel and the wings are shown as halves. Hem along the trailing edges and along the side of the apron. Now join the wings in the normal way, then make casings for the leading edge spars. Mark the sewing-line for the keel.

Cut out the keel and hem the top and bottom edges. Using a domestic iron press it along the centre line and make a seam 8 mm ($\frac{5}{16}$ inch) from the fold. Fit an eyelet or sew a tape loop at the tip, then sew the keel in place on each wing (Fig 7.15).

Fit spreader bar connections 43 cm (17 inches) from the wing tip. Fit the spine, spars and spreader in the usual manner.

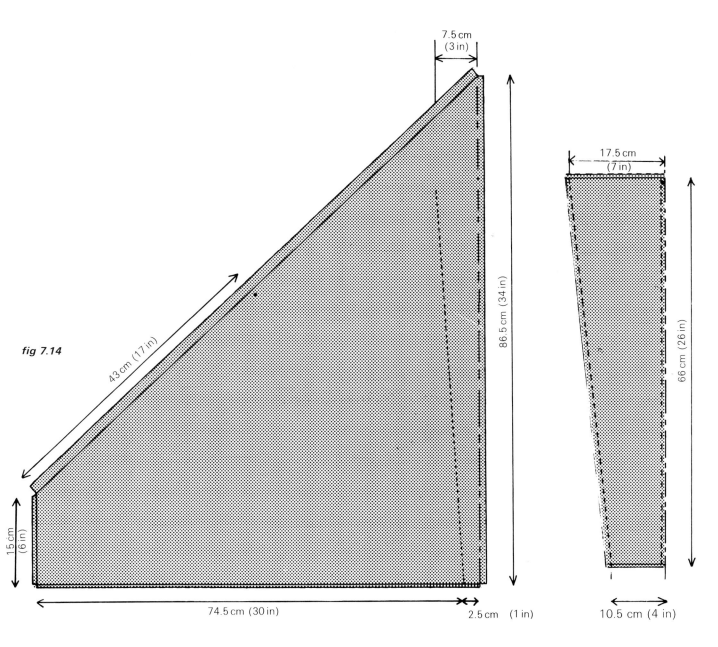

fig 7.14

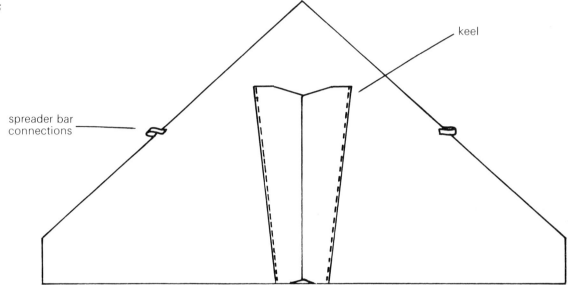

fig 7.15

spreader bar
connections

keel

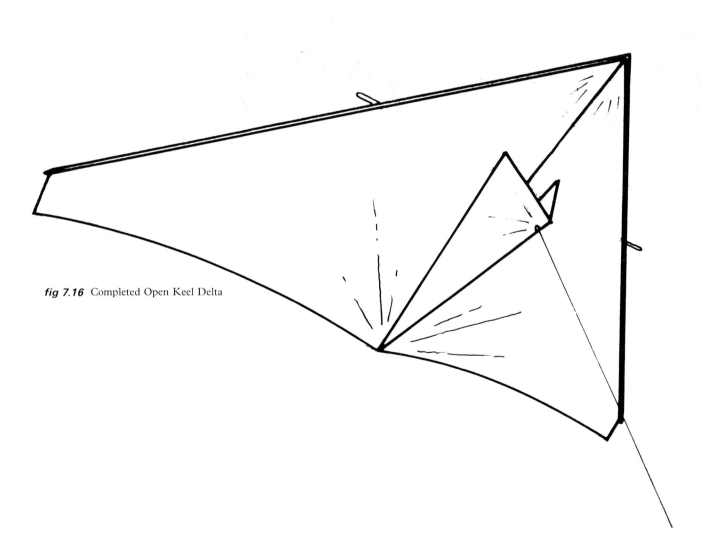

fig 7.16 Completed Open Keel Delta

SAIL KITE (TREFOIL)

Sail   : Polycotton, nylon taffeta (not
                  spinnaker rip-stop)
Spars   : 6.4 mm ($\frac{1}{4}$ inch) dowel. Spine
                  (Beech) 93 cm (37 inches)
                  Leading edge (Ramin)
                  2 pieces 87 cm ($34\frac{1}{4}$ inches)
                  Spreader bar (Ramin) to fit
Tail   : Tailless
Line   : 15 kg (33 lb)
Wind speed   : Light–moderate
Time to make   : 2–3 hrs
Difficulty   : ★★★

Make the template according to Fig 7.18 and cut out the two wing pieces; weave in the direction shown.

Make casing for leading edge spars, join the wings and create a spine-casing in the standard manner.

Fold the wings back to back, then mark and sew along the lines according to the pattern to create cambered aerofoil shape (Fig 7.19).

Fit spreader connections 60 cm (24 inches) from the wing tip. Fit the spine, leading edge spars and spreader bar. A point not always appreciated by some kitemakers, and which Helen takes pains to point out, is that spreader bar is much shorter than it would be in the standard delta, so that wings form a dihedral angle of approximately 165 degrees.

The line is connected directly to the keel from a point 45 cm (18 inches) from the base.

Design reproduced with permission from *Make mine fly* by Helen Bushell.

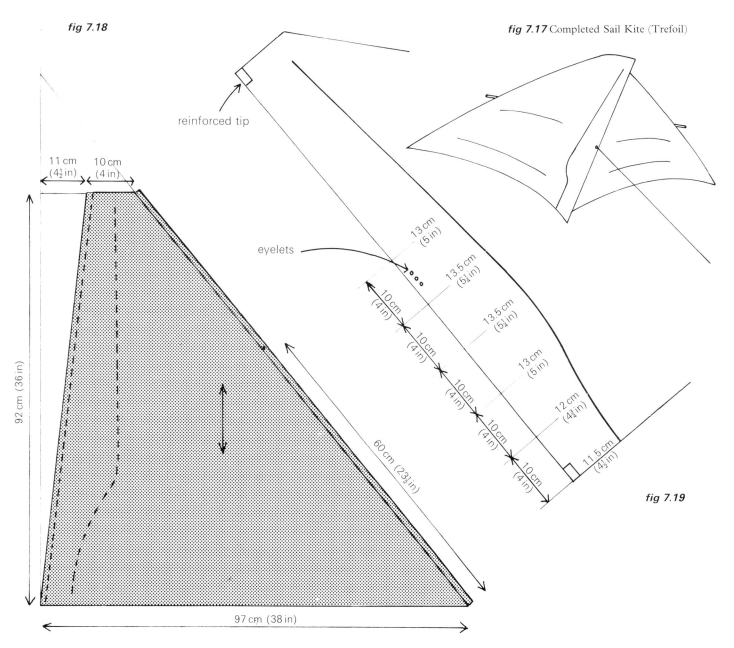

fig 7.18

fig 7.17 Completed Sail Kite (Trefoil)

fig 7.19

Sail	: Rip-stop nylon
Spars	: Ramin Dowel. Spine 12 mm ($\frac{1}{2}$ inch) × 127 cm (50 inches) Leading edge spars 2 pieces 10 mm ($\frac{3}{8}$ inch) × 140 cm (55 inches) Spreader 12 mm ($\frac{1}{2}$ inch) × 117 cm ($46\frac{1}{2}$ inches) (approx)
Tail	: Tailless
Line	: 35 kg (77 lb)
Wind speeds	: Light–gentle
Time to make	: 4–6 hrs
Difficulty	: ★★★★

Cut out wing pieces, shown here as halves, and the keel (Fig 7.20). As the trailing edge has this rather sharp scallop, it is probably better to edge-bind rather than attempt to hem it.

Join the wings and create casings for the spine and leading edge spars in the standard manner. Mark sewing lines for the keel piece.

Fit the keel piece to the rear of the kite along the sewing lines previously marked. Making the apex of the triangle fit neatly together is something which might prove difficult, so think it through very carefully before you start stitching.

The original design had a two-leg bridle to points equidistant (40 cm) (16 inches) from the tip and base of the spine. In Jerry Sinnote's more recent version, however, he has chosen to fit a very narrow ventral keel, which would slightly improve stability but more importantly provide a convenient attachment point for the flying line. I much prefer a narrow keel, 7.5 cm (3 inches) wide with a tip 44 cm ($17\frac{1}{2}$ inches) from the spine tip.

Fit spreader bar connections 101.5 cm (40 inches) from the wing tips, then leading edge spars, spine and spreader in the normal way.

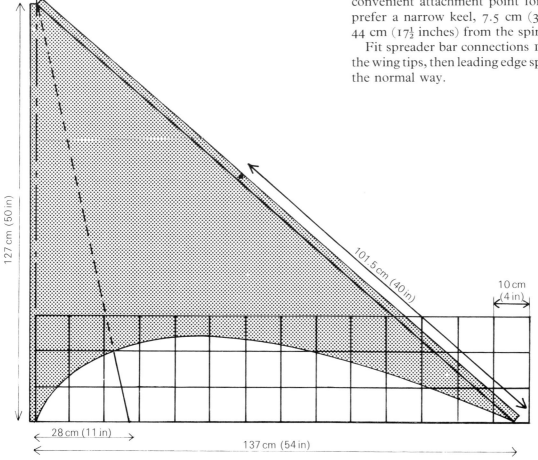

fig 7.20 (a)

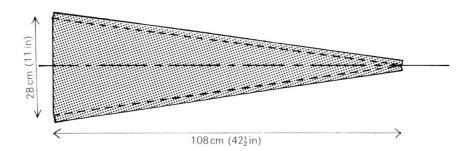

fig 7.20 (b)

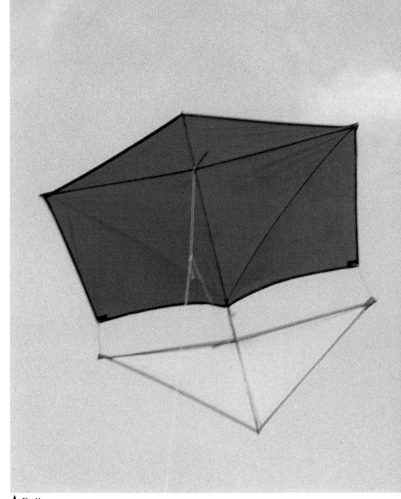

▲White dove

▼Rogallo corner kite   ▲Roller   ▼Pentacorn

▲ Mini flexikite (Tyvek) ▲ Starflake ▼ Extended keel delta

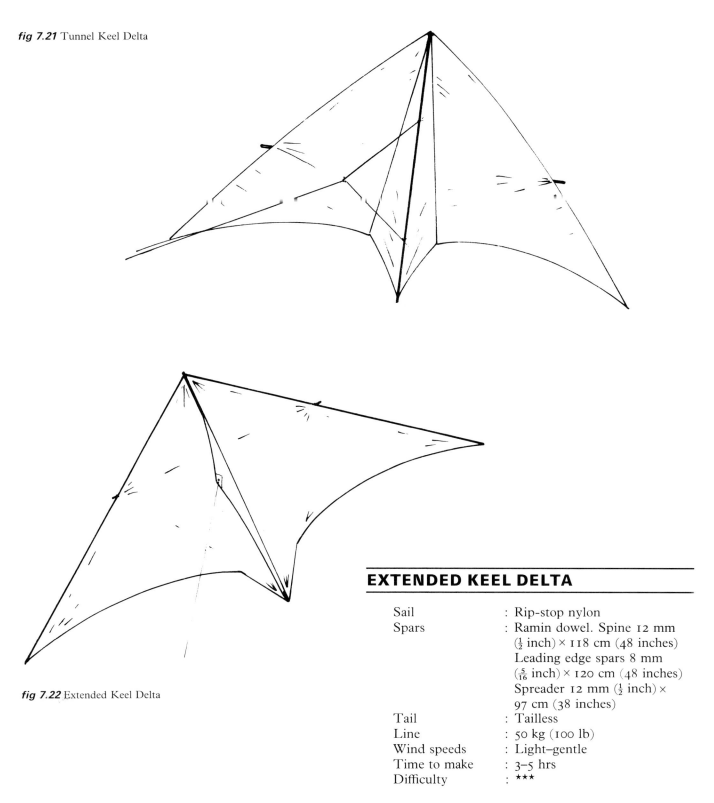

fig 7.21 Tunnel Keel Delta

fig 7.22 Extended Keel Delta

EXTENDED KEEL DELTA

Sail	:	Rip-stop nylon
Spars	:	Ramin dowel. Spine 12 mm ($\frac{1}{2}$ inch) × 118 cm (48 inches) Leading edge spars 8 mm ($\frac{5}{16}$ inch) × 120 cm (48 inches) Spreader 12 mm ($\frac{1}{2}$ inch) × 97 cm (38 inches)
Tail	:	Tailless
Line	:	50 kg (100 lb)
Wind speeds	:	Light–gentle
Time to make	:	3–5 hrs
Difficulty	:	★★★

A high aspect-ratio wing with just a hint of a tail.

Make the templates according to the pattern (Fig 7.23) and cut out the two wings and keel. Make the keel with hems along two sides and fit eyelets or tape loops as preferred.

Make casings for leading edge spars and join the wings in the standard manner, creating the forward casing for the spine.

Fit spreader bar connections 84 cm (33$\frac{1}{2}$ inches) from the wing tips. Add leading edge spars, spine and spreader.

65

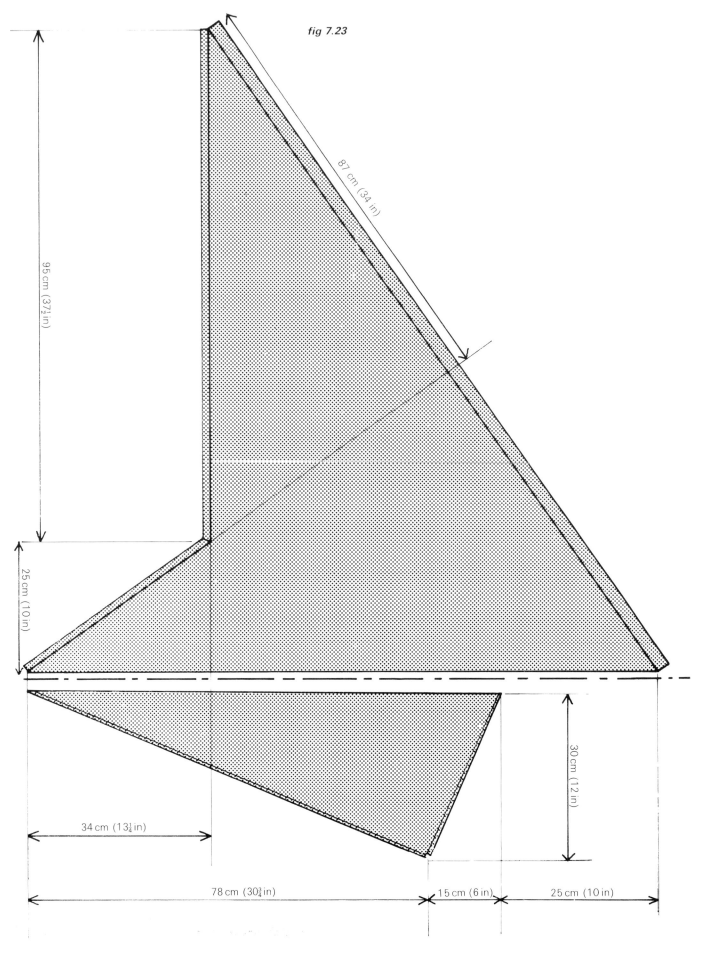

fig 7.23

95 cm (37½ in)

25 cm (10 in)

87 cm (34 in)

30 cm (12 in)

34 cm (13¼ in)

78 cm (30¾ in)

15 cm (6 in)

25 cm (10 in)

CHAPTER EIGHT

corner kites

For those who like designs with a geometric simplicity, then both corner kites and their cousins the facets are ideal.

SINGLE-CELL CORNER KITES

The corner kite has been described as an 'inside out' box kite, and looking at its basic shape you can perhaps see why. The single cell is made up of two squares joined along the diagonal to create four externally-braced 45-degree triangular sails.

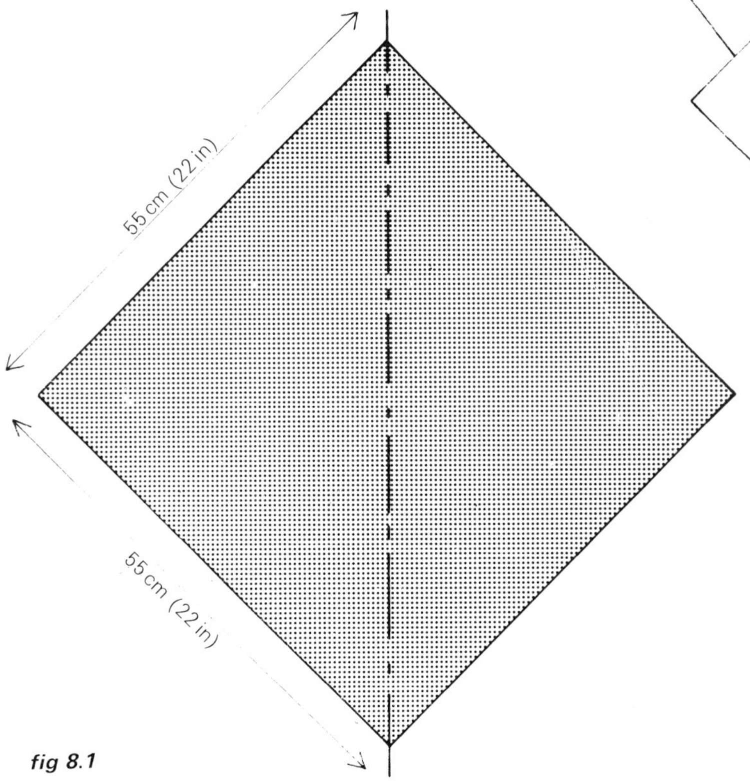

fig 8.1

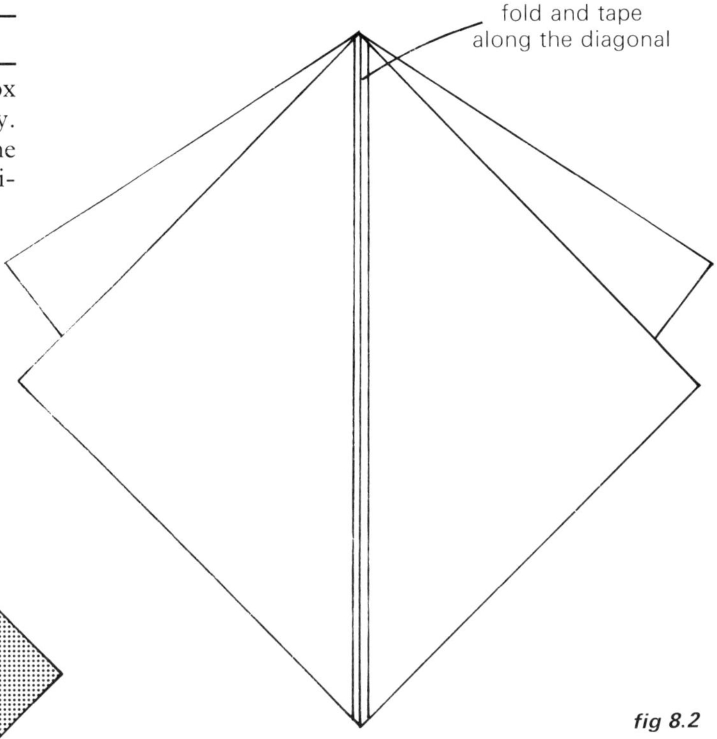

fold and tape along the diagonal

fig 8.2

Sail	: Polythene, Tyvek
Spars	: Ramin dowel. Spine 6.4 mm ($\frac{1}{4}$ inch) × approximately 80 cm ($31\frac{1}{2}$ inches) Bracing spars 4 pieces 6.4 mm ($\frac{1}{4}$ inch) × approximately 57 cm (22 inches)
Other materials	: 6.4 mm ($\frac{1}{4}$ inch) PVC tube. 6 × 12 mm ($\frac{1}{2}$ inch) split rings
Line	: 10 kg (20 lb)
Tail	: Small drogue/ribbon tail
Wind speed	: Light–moderate
Time to make	: 1 hr
Difficulty	: ★★

From the template (Fig 8.1) cut out two squares of material, side length 55 cm (22 inches). You can use a larger square, say 60–70 cm (24–32 inches), if you wish, but as explained below it is unwise to make it much smaller unless you also reduce the weight of the spars.

Fold each square along the diagonal and tape them together (Fig 8.2). Next make spar connections, fitted using fabric tape, to the base and tip of the kite and to the four wing tips as in Fig 8.3. Carefully fit the spine and bracing spars, ensuring the sail is evenly tensioned. Do also be sure to make all the bracing spars exactly the same length.

This particular method of construction requires the use of a three-leg bridle as shown. The two lower bridle legs should each be between one and one and a half times the size of square used, in this case 80 cm (32 inches) long. The upper bridle leg is usually fitted with a slider and attached to the spine 15 cm (6 inches) from the tip.

Small corner kites are notoriously unstable and the ratio of weight to sail area seems to be quite critical. In light winds if the towing point is set low, to get it airborne, you will find that the corner kite is unstable; set it higher and it won't lift. Tails are consequently almost always required.

In some workshops, to overcome the problem of instability, I often use an alternative sail shape (Fig 8.5).

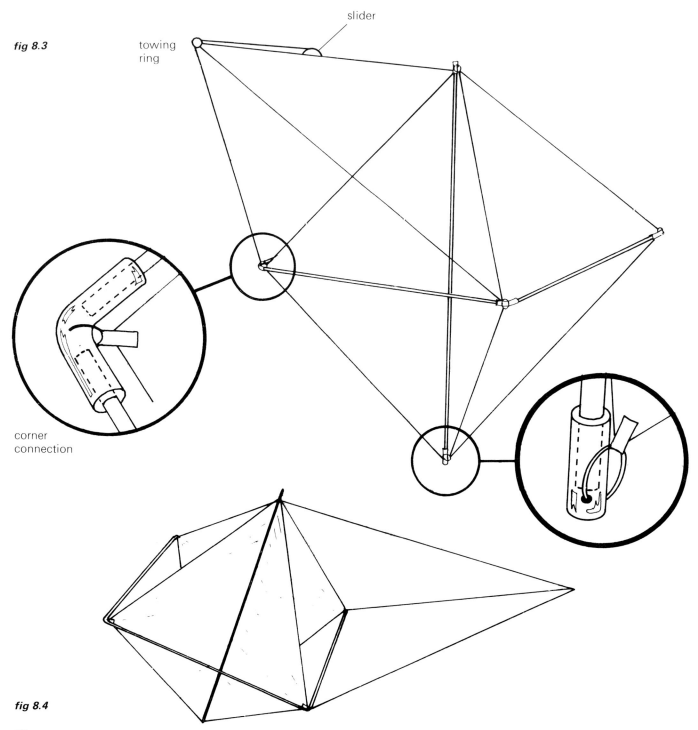

fig 8.3

slider

towing ring

corner connection

fig 8.4

68

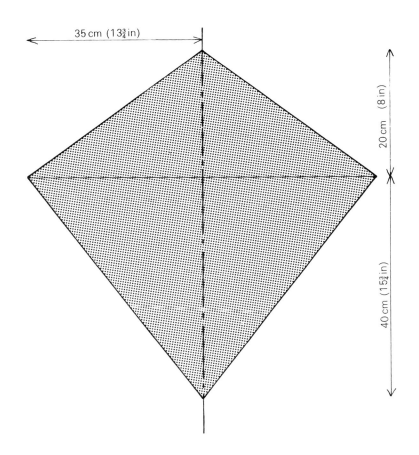

fig 8.5

SIX-WING CORNER KITE

Sail	:	Tyvek, strong wrapping paper
Spars	:	Ramin dowel. Spine 6.4 mm ($\frac{1}{4}$ inch) × approximately 62 cm (25 inches)
		Bracing spars 6 pieces 6.4 mm ($\frac{1}{4}$ inch) × approximately 52 cm (21 inches)
Other materials	:	6.4 mm ($\frac{1}{4}$ inch) PVC tube; 8 × 12 mm ($\frac{1}{4}$ inch) split rings
Tail	:	Tape 2–3 metres (6–10 feet)
Line	:	15 kg (35 lb)
Wind Speed	:	Light–gentle
Time to make	:	1 hr
Difficulty	:	★

The template for this design is an equilateral triangle of 60 cm (24 inches) sides (Fig 8.6). As with the four-wing corner kite, the wing size can of course be scaled up or down, within reasonable limits.

Lay the template edge along a fold in the material and cut through two layers, to produce a diamond shape. You will

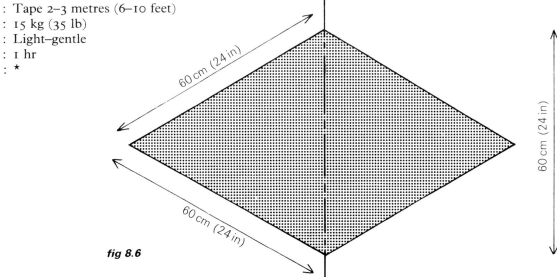

fig 8.6

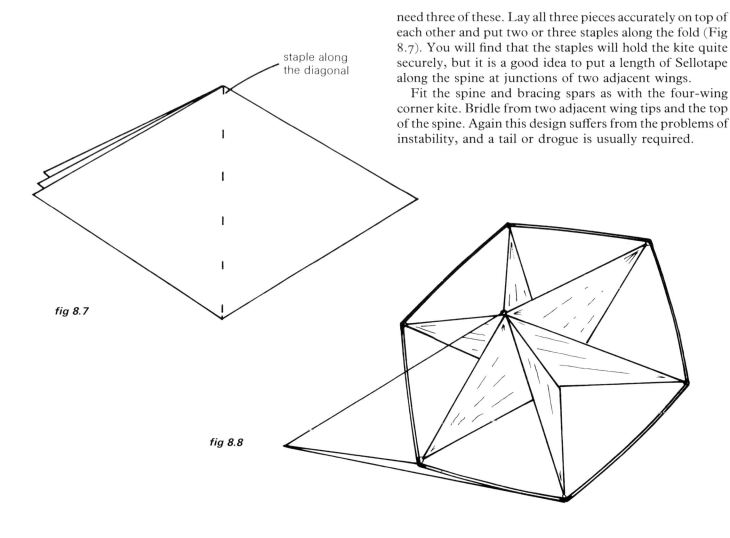

staple along the diagonal

fig 8.7

fig 8.8

need three of these. Lay all three pieces accurately on top of each other and put two or three staples along the fold (Fig 8.7). You will find that the staples will hold the kite quite securely, but it is a good idea to put a length of Sellotape along the spine at junctions of two adjacent wings.

Fit the spine and bracing spars as with the four-wing corner kite. Bridle from two adjacent wing tips and the top of the spine. Again this design suffers from the problems of instability, and a tail or drogue is usually required.

ROGALLO CORNER KITE

In creating a multi-cell version you have two options: to set the cells side by side, or, as the Rogallo Corner kite, two cells set one on top of the other on a single spine.

Sail : Rip-stop nylon
Spars : Ramin dowel. Spine 10 mm ($\frac{3}{8}$ inch) approx 215 cm (87 inches) Bracing spars 8 mm ($\frac{5}{16}$ inch) 8 pieces approx 77 cm (30 inches)
Other materials : 10 × 15 mm ($\frac{3}{8}$ inch) split rings. 8 sliders PVC tube 10 mm ($\frac{3}{8}$ inch) and 8 mm ($\frac{5}{16}$ inch)
Line : 25 kg (50 lb)
Tail : Tailless
Wind speed : Light–moderate
Time to make : 2–3 hrs
Difficulty : ★★★

Make a square template as indicated in Fig 8.9.

Cut out four pieces of fabric with the weave parallel to the edge and hem, or bind to create 75 cm (30 inch) squares. Make two corner cells by joining pairs of wings together with broad tapes along the diagonal in two rows of stitching approximately 17 mm ($\frac{3}{4}$ inch) apart. The tape should also be formed into loops at the top and bottom of each cell (Fig 8.10).

Sew short loops to the wing tips. Ensure they are of equal length and evenly sewn.

Next fit the spine into the casing created along the diagonals and join the loops between the cells with a short length of line, which also secures the sails to the spine at the centre.

Fit the tube connectors at the tip and base of the kite and trim the spine to fit tightly. Now fit corner connections, add the spars as indicated and ensure that the sails are taut but evenly tensioned. To prevent cells from twisting you should now fit bracing lines with sliders to opposite corners (Fig 8.11).

The flying line is attached direct to any corner.

This model sits at a seeming high angle of attack, but is nonetheless quite stable over a range of wind speeds.

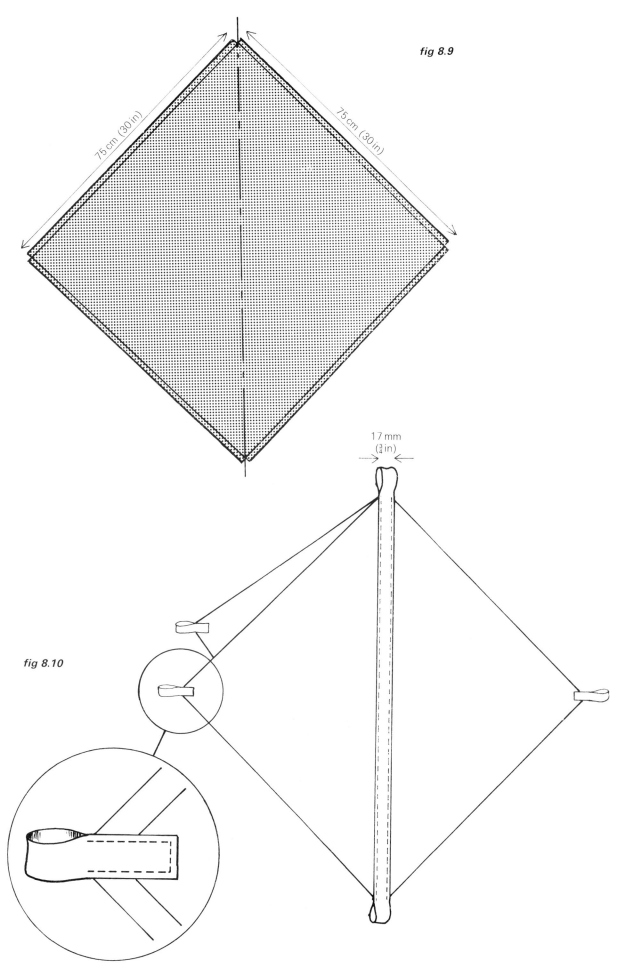

fig 8.9

75 cm (30 in)

75 cm (30 in)

17 mm
(¾ in)

fig 8.10

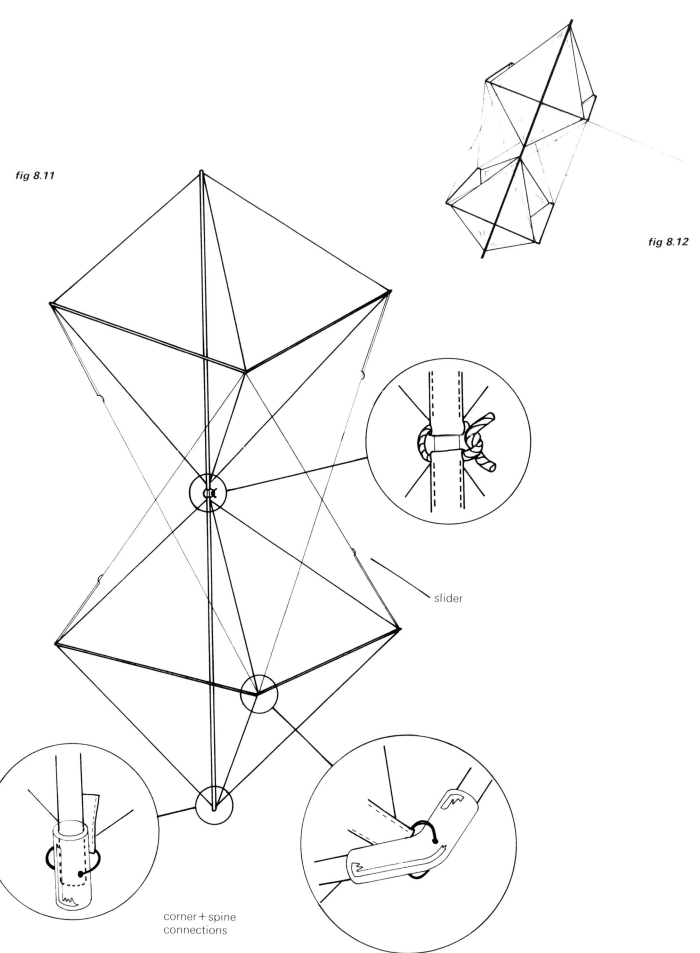

fig 8.11

fig 8.12

slider

corner + spine
connections

PENTACORN

It is possible to go on combining either single or double cells as above, although structures beyond three or four are sometimes awkward to fly. The Pentacorn is an interesting combination of cells which, although not terribly easy to construct, is extremely satisfying to fly.

Sail	: Rip-stop nylon
Spars	: Ramin dowel. Spines 8 mm ($\frac{5}{16}$ inch) 5 pieces approx 78 cm (31 inches) Bracing spars 8 mm ($\frac{5}{16}$ inch) 5 pieces approx 82 cm (32$\frac{1}{2}$ inches)
Other materials	: PVC tube 8 mm ($\frac{5}{16}$ inch) 15 × 12 mm ($\frac{1}{2}$ inch) split rings 10 × 15 mm ($\frac{5}{8}$ inch) split rings
Line	: 50 kg (100 lb)
Wind speed	: Gentle–moderate
Time to make	: 6–8 hrs
Difficulty	: ****

This basic sail shape is not a square but a diamond 76 cm (30 inches) long, 60 cm (24 inches) wide.

Cut out 10 diamonds and 5 triangles and mark sewing lines *AB*, *CD* as indicated (Fig 8.13 (a), (b)). Join the shapes, two diamonds and one triangle, along the diagonal *AB* to create five five-winged cells. Reinforce the seam with a narrow tape, also creating loops at the tip and base as with previous corner kites.

Now join the cells together by sewing two of the wings of adjacent cells along *CD*. You should end up with five cells, each having three external and two internal wings, the latter sewn to its neighbour on the adjacent cell (Fig 8.14).

Sew tape loops to the five corner wing-tips and fit corner connections. The remaining wings are joined to their neighbours of the next cell at the tips, enclosing a short tape loop between. Similarly, join pairs of adjacent inner wing tips, again enclosing tape loops to create the pattern indicated in Fig 8.15. Thread a small split ring through each of these loops and fit spine connections.

Now carefully fit the spines and bracing spars into the corner connections and through the rings at intermediate

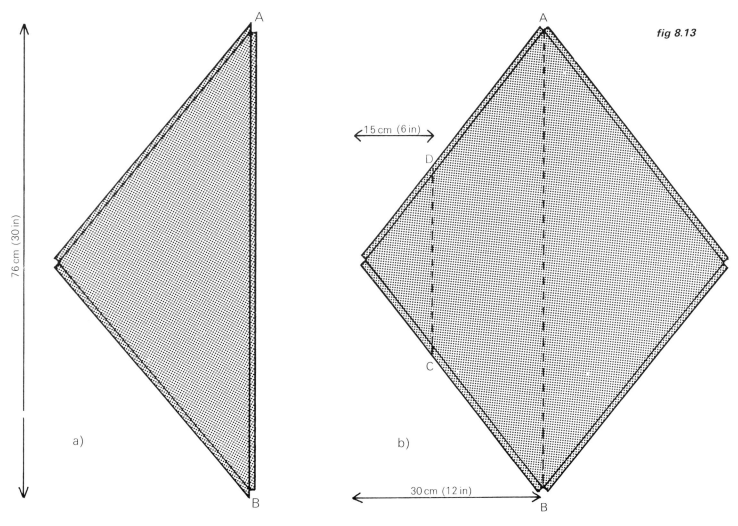

fig 8.13

wing pairs. Both should be trimmed so that the sails are tight but evenly tensioned.

Join the pairs of inner wing-tips with a line threaded through each loop to make a pentangle. Make a four-leg bridle, each leg approximately 1.5 metres (5 feet) long, from two spine-tips and two corner wing-tips on the same side. Additional bracing lines may also be attached in loops joining spine tips and bases. Adjust the bridles to create a suitable angle of attack.

The Pentacorn sits at quite a high angle of attack, and can pull quite hard in more moderate conditions. In lighter, steadier winds, however, it flies like a dream.

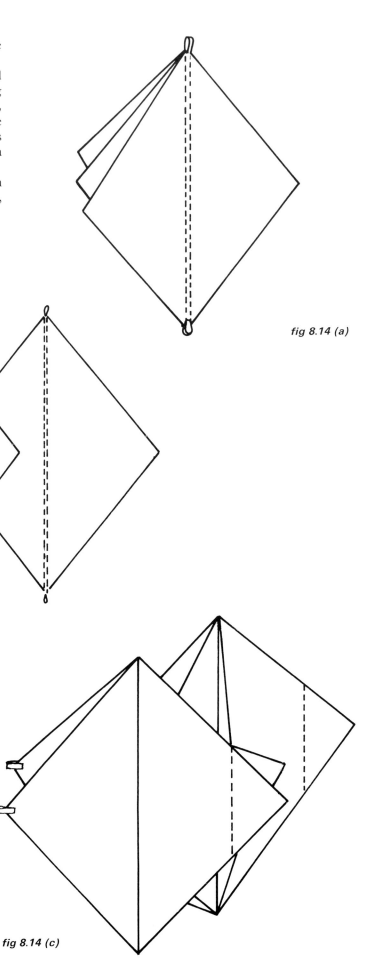

fig 8.14 (a)

fig 8.14 (b)

fig 8.14 (c)

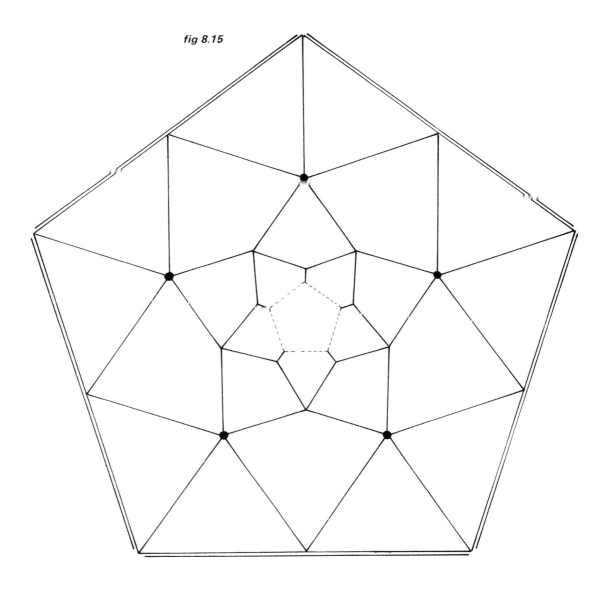

fig 8.15

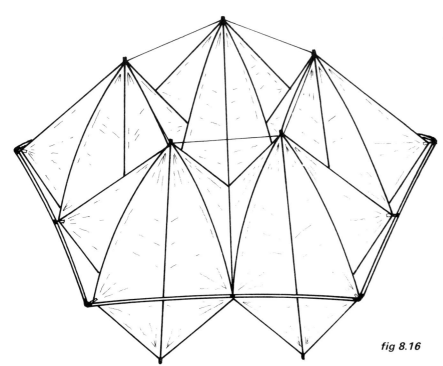

fig 8.16

QUAD

Another interesting variation on the multiple-corner kite, here using four cells around a central square box.

Sail	: Rip-stop nylon
Spars	: Ramin dowel. Spines 6.4 mm ($\frac{5}{16}$ inch) 4 pieces approximately 78 cm (31 inches) Bracing spars 8 mm ($\frac{5}{16}$ inch) 4 pieces approx 88 cm (34$\frac{1}{2}$ inches)
Other materials	: PVC tube 8 mm ($\frac{5}{16}$ inch) Split rings 16 × 15 mm ($\frac{5}{8}$ inch)
Line	: 35 kg (75 lb)
Wind speed	: Light–moderate
Time to make	: 6–8 hrs
Difficulty	: ★★★

The template for this design is the same as the Pentacorn. You will, however, need just 8 diamonds plus 4 additional pieces of sail which after hemming/binding on two sides only are 22.5 × 38 cm (9 × 15 inches) (Fig 8.17).

The Quad is made up of just four four-winged cells, but instead of the wings being joined to each other, they are joined via the additional sail pieces which together form a central square box.

Sew the diamonds in pairs along the diagonal, and reinforce with tape as above to create the four cells. Mark the sewing line *CD* on one wing of each cell. Sew the squares in position along this line, joining the cells at the same time (Fig 8.18).

Sew a tape loop to each of the four outer corner wing-tips and to the inner tips. Join the remaining wings of adjacent cells in pairs at the tips, enclosing a short tape loop as above.

Fit spine end and corner connections, and rings to the loops of intermediate pairs of wings. Next fit the spines and

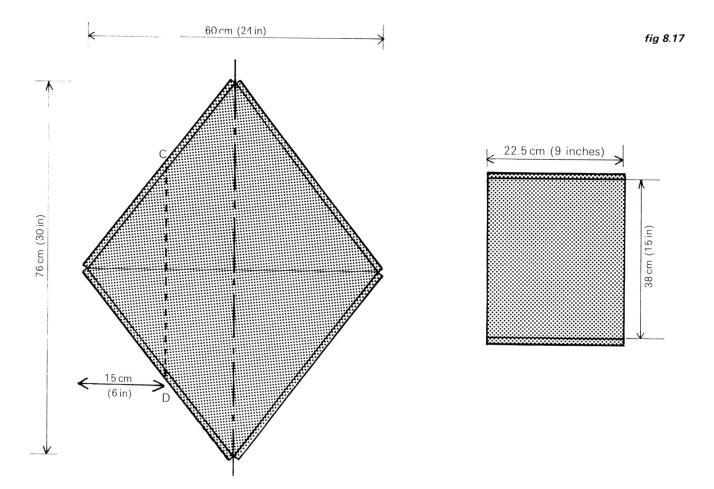

fig 8.17

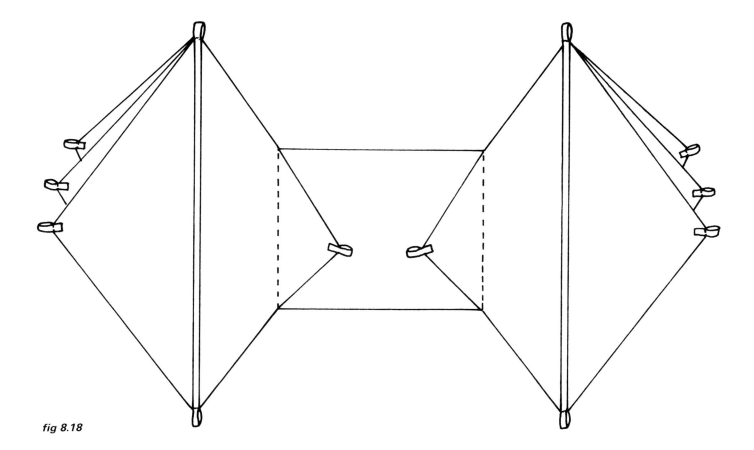

fig 8.18

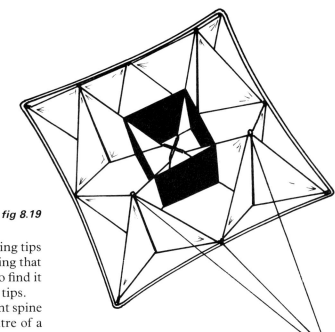

fig 8.19

spars as with previous corner kites and tie central wing tips to their opposite numbers with a loop of line, ensuring that the sails are taut but evenly tensioned. You may also find it useful to add bracing lines joining opposite spine tips.

Tie a three-leg bridle, two legs taken from adjacent spine tips and a third from the wing junction at the centre of a bracing spar (Fig 8.19).

As it has such a high aspect-ratio, the Quad seems to fly at a very high angle of attack – almost vertical – but because of the sail configuration it is in fact very low and it flies with beautiful stability.

PETER LYNN BOX KITE

The Peter Lynn box kite is usually based on a square-shaped wing, but more recently designers have been using wings based on 60-degree triangles, as here.

Sail	: Rip-stop nylon
Spars	: Ramin dowel. 8 mm ($\frac{5}{16}$ inch) Spines 2 pieces approx 125 cm (50 inches) Bracing spars 4 pieces approx 91 cm (36 inches) 4 pieces approx 38 cm (15 inches)
Other materials	: 20–35 SWG 8 mm ($\frac{5}{16}$ inch) internal aluminium tube or similar brass 4 × 12 cm (5 inches) to create 4-way joint
Tail	: Tailless
Line	: 40 kg (90 lb)
Wind Speed	: Light–gentle
Time to make	: 6–8 hrs
Difficulty	: ★★★

Cut out four diamond and four triangular wings which after hemming/binding are of 60 cm (24 inch) sides (Fig 18.20). Cut a small hole in one side of each of the triangles and reinforce it by fixing an additional piece of fabric in place and sewing two small semicircles.

To make up each cell, sew the triangles along the diagonals of the diamonds in a single row of stitching, and reinforce the seam with narrow (8 mm) ($\frac{5}{16}$ inch) binding tape, making loops at the top and bottom. Also sew short tape loops at the tips (Fig 18.21).

The cells are then joined in pairs on each spine (Fig 18.22). In the figure tube and ring connections are shown but any other suitable connections can of course be used.

Normally the central 'box' is a square, but the relative angles of the wings can be altered to create a diamond, for example, thereby altering the kite's flying characteristics slightly.

To create this central square, dimensions have to be worked out mathematically, as indicated in Fig 18.23.

As with previous corner kites, the spars should be trimmed so that the sails are taut and evenly tensioned.

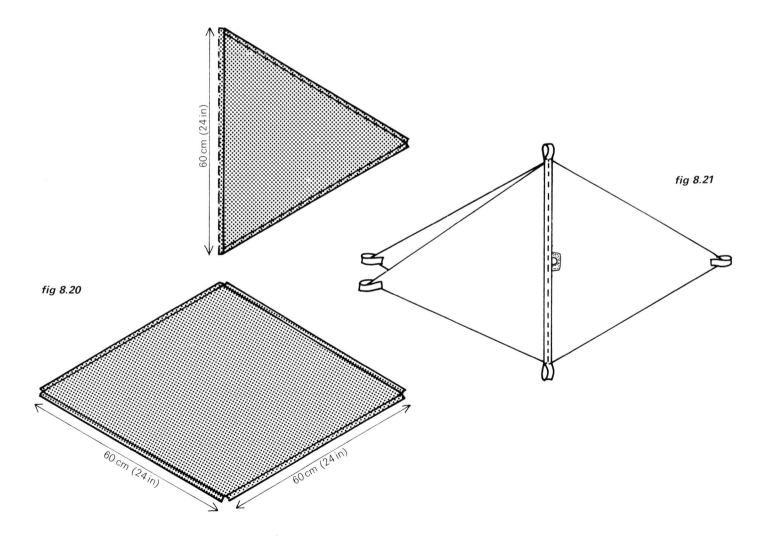

fig 8.20

fig 8.21

The flying-line is taken directly from a forward sail junction.

Peter Lynn box kites generally have a very strong pull in comparison to their size. If you've never flown one before, be prepared for a surprise.

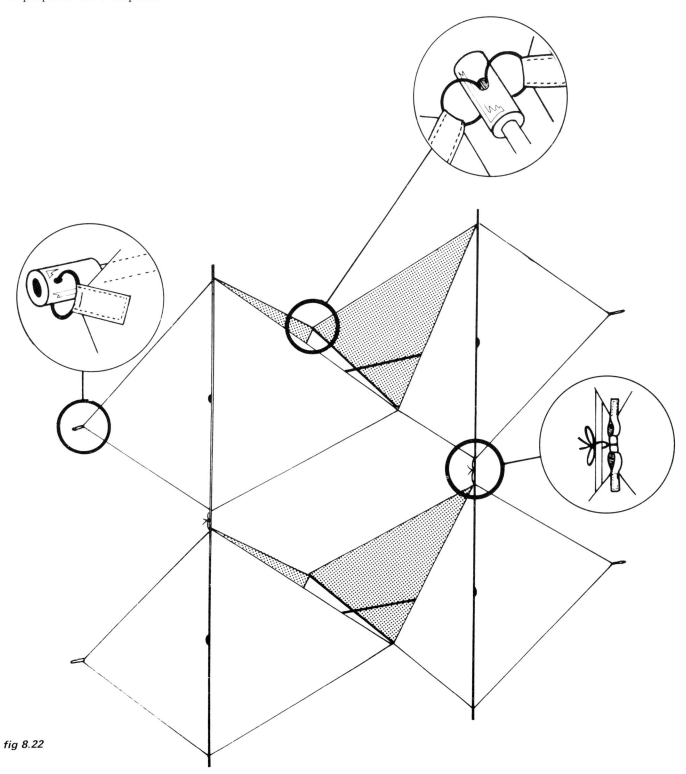

fig 8.22

fig 8.23

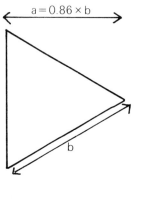

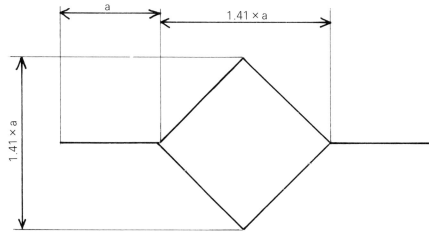

fig 8.24

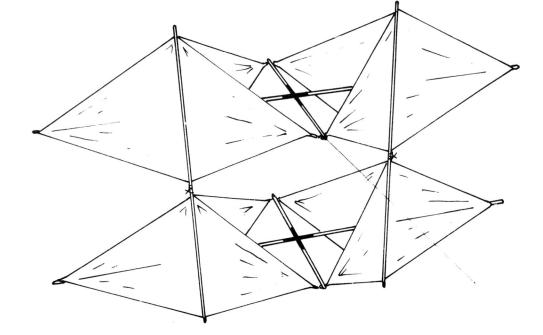

SPUTNIK

Sail	: Rip-stop nylon
Spars	: Ramin dowel. Spine 8 mm ($\frac{5}{16}$ inch) × approx 155 cm (61 inches) Bracing spars 6.4 mm ($\frac{1}{4}$ inch) 6 pieces approx 77 cm (30$\frac{1}{2}$ inches)
Other materials	: PVC tube 8 mm ($\frac{5}{16}$ inch) and 6.4 mm ($\frac{1}{4}$ inch) Split rings 2 × 15 mm ($\frac{5}{8}$ inch) 6 × 12 mm ($\frac{1}{2}$ inch)
Tail	: Tailless
Line	: 35 kg (75 lb)
Wind speed	: Gentle–moderate
Time to make	: 6–8 hrs
Difficulty	: ★★★

Draw a 45-degree triangle with 75 cm (30 inch) side and from this mark out the trapezoidal shape shown, making allowances for hems on two sides only (Fig 8.25). Cut out twelve pieces of fabric with the weave in the direction shown, and mark sewing lines.

Cut out an additional twelve pieces of fabric which, after hemming on two opposite sides only, will be 25 cm (10 inches) square.

Join the large sail pieces together using a modular sail construction as described in Chapter 5 with tapes also creating loops at both ends, to make up six pairs (Fig 8.26). Then combine all six pairs together, again creating loops at both ends (Fig 8.27).

Sew the smaller squares in place along the lines previously drawn to create a central hexagon box (Fig 8.28).

Fit corner tubes and spine end connections. Cut and fit the spine and bracing spars such that the sail is evenly tensioned throughout. Finally, tie bracing lines joining opposite loops within the central 'hole'.

To fly the Sputnik tie a three-leg bridle to the spine tip and two adjacent wing-tips as with previous corner kites.

The Sputnik likes steady winds, but in turbulent conditions a coloured, long tubular tail will help keep it stable while adding some sparkle to its dance.

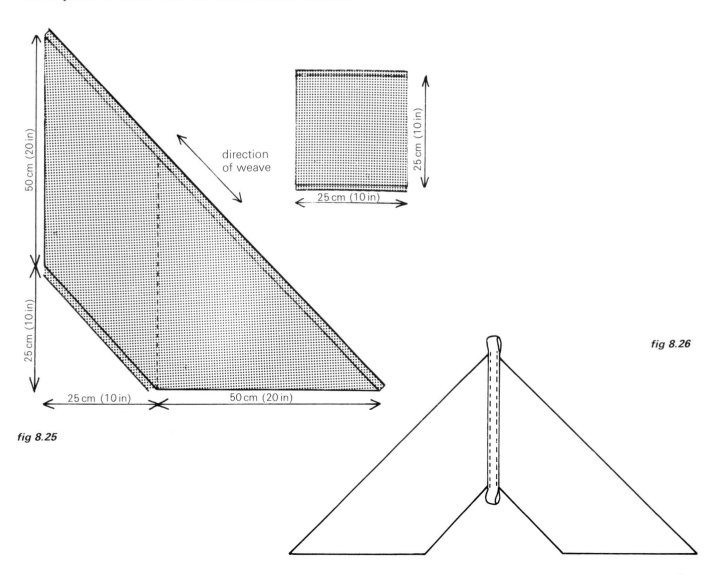

direction of weave

25 cm (10 in)

25 cm (10 in)

fig 8.26

50 cm (20 in)

25 cm (10 in)

25 cm (10 in)

50 cm (20 in)

fig 8.25

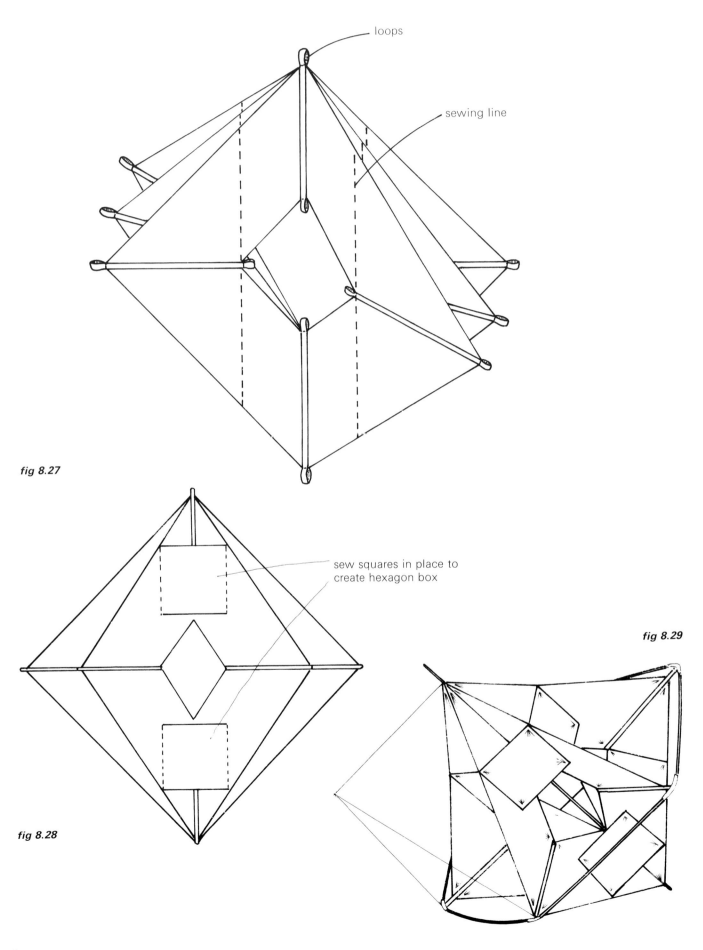

loops

sewing line

fig 8.27

sew squares in place to
create hexagon box

fig 8.29

fig 8.28

facet kites

POLYTHENE FACET

This is a simple facet which I originally tried in workshops with a Sellotape construction, but found that the joints gradually pulled apart and it really must be welded.

Sails	: 300 gauge Polythene
Spars	: 6.4 mm ($\frac{1}{4}$ inch) Ramin dowel. Spine approx 86 cm ($31\frac{1}{2}$ inches) Bracing spars 4 pieces approx 62 cm (25 inches)
Other materials	: 6.4 mm ($\frac{1}{4}$ inch) PVC tube Split rings 6 × 12 mm ($\frac{1}{2}$ inch), 4 × 8 mm ($\frac{5}{16}$ inch) Slider
Tail	: Ribbon tail/drogue
Line	: 15 kg (35 lb)

Wind speed	: Light–gentle
Time to make	: 1 hr
Difficulty	: ★★

Cut out two squares of polythene 60 cm (24 inch) side. Weld them together along the diagonal *AB* as though you were making a single cell corner kite (Figs 9.1, 9.2).

Now cut out four small squares of 30 cm (12 inch) sides, crease and weld them along the diagonal onto the larger wings along *CE* as illustrated (Fig 9.3). Fit spar tubes to each of the four corner wing-tips and to the spine-tip and base then join pairs of inner wings with a small piece of fabric tape and a small ring.

Fit the spine and thread the spars through the rings and into the corner connections. The sails should be tight but evenly tensioned.

Fit a three-leg bridle as with the corner kite, although the upper leg can be taken from the spine tip if preferred.

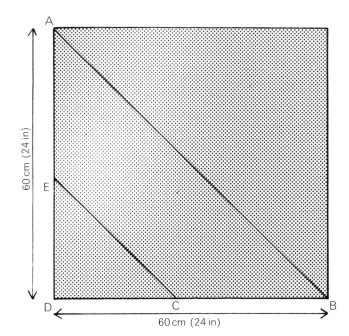

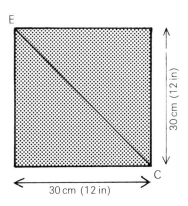

fig 9.1

fig 9.2

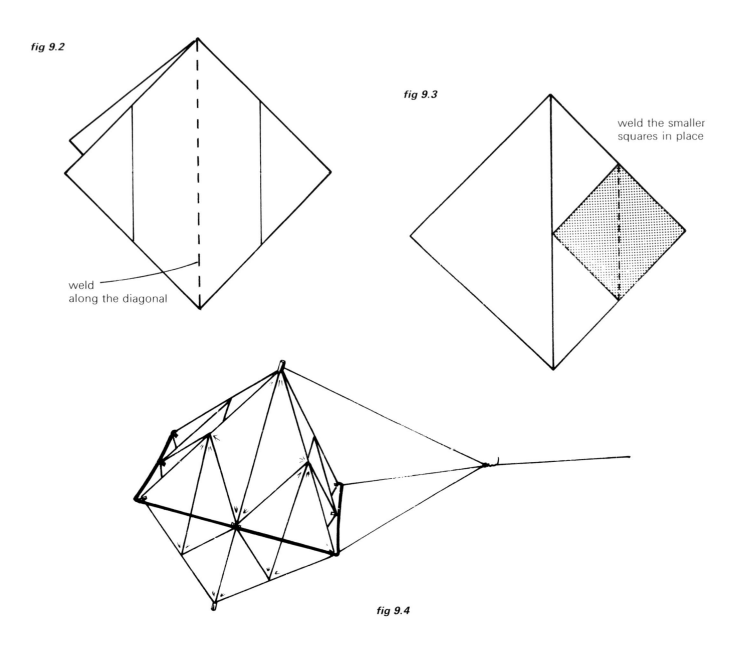

weld
along the diagonal

fig 9.3

weld the smaller
squares in place

fig 9.4

FABRIC FIVE-SIDED FACET

Sail	:	Rip-stop nylon
Spars	:	Ramin dowel. Spine 10 mm ($\frac{3}{8}$ inch) × 110 cm (44 inches) Bracing spars 8 mm ($\frac{5}{16}$ inch) × approximately 64 cm (25 inches)
Other materials	:	PVC Tube 10 mm ($\frac{3}{8}$ inch) and 8 mm ($\frac{5}{16}$ inch). Split rings 2 × 20 mm ($\frac{3}{4}$ inch), 5 × 15 mm ($\frac{5}{8}$ inch), 10 × 12 mm ($\frac{1}{2}$ inch) Slider
Tail	:	Tailless
Line	:	35 kg (75 lb)
Wind Speed	:	Light–moderate
Time to Make	:	6–8 hrs
Difficulty	:	★★★★

Make the templates as indicated adding suitable amounts for hemming/binding as preferred and use them to create two large squares of fabric of 75 cm sides (30 inch); one 45-degree triangle 75 cm (30 inch) side; 5 squares 50 cm (20 inches) side and 5 squares 25 cm (10 inches) side. Mark sewing lines on all the shapes as indicated (Fig 9.5).

Sew the two largest squares together along the diagonal with the triangle sandwiched between to create the five-winged cell. Reinforce the seam using a length of a narrow tape in two close rows of stitching with loops at the tip and base (Fig 9.6).

Sew the smaller squares in place on each of the wings, first the 50 cm (20 inch) squares, then the 25 cm (10 inch) squares (Fig 9.7). Then join the intermediate (50 cm) wings in pairs along the sewing lines indicated to create the first stage of the snowflake (Fig 9.8).

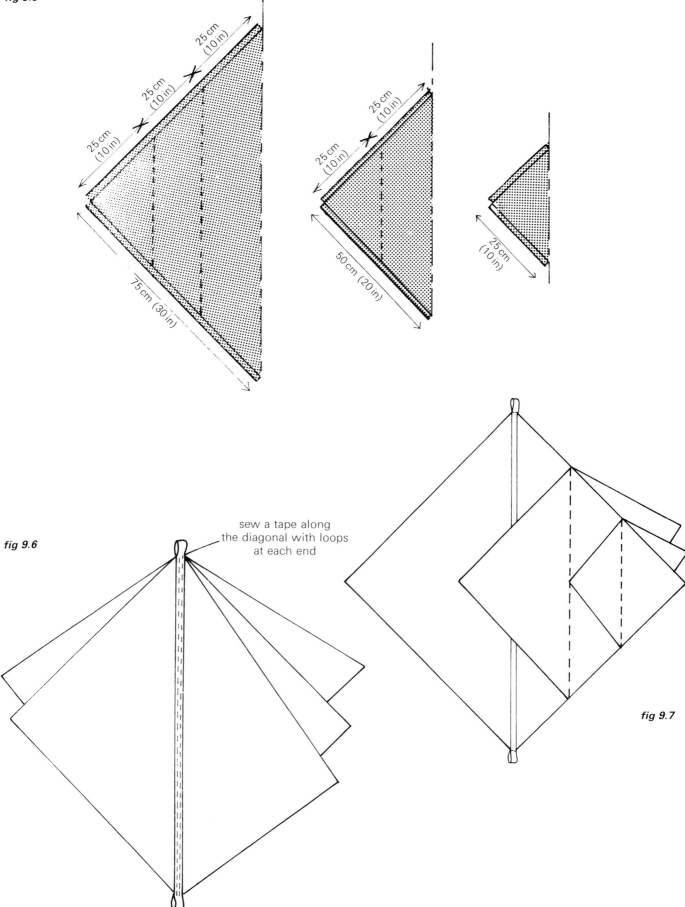

fig 9.5

25 cm (10 in)

25 cm (10 in)

25 cm (10 in)

75 cm (30 in)

25 cm (10 in)

25 cm (10 in)

50 cm (20 in)

25 cm (10 in)

fig 9.6

sew a tape along
the diagonal with loops
at each end

fig 9.7

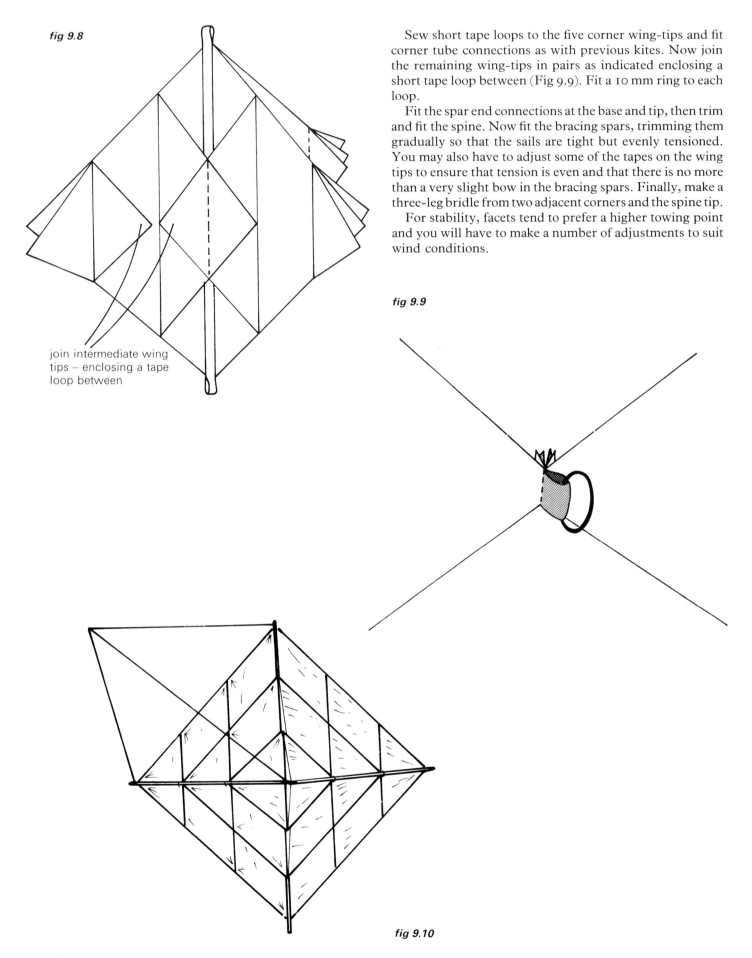

fig 9.8

join intermediate wing
tips – enclosing a tape
loop between

Sew short tape loops to the five corner wing-tips and fit corner tube connections as with previous kites. Now join the remaining wing-tips in pairs as indicated enclosing a short tape loop between (Fig 9.9). Fit a 10 mm ring to each loop.

Fit the spar end connections at the base and tip, then trim and fit the spine. Now fit the bracing spars, trimming them gradually so that the sails are tight but evenly tensioned. You may also have to adjust some of the tapes on the wing tips to ensure that tension is even and that there is no more than a very slight bow in the bracing spars. Finally, make a three-leg bridle from two adjacent corners and the spine tip.

For stability, facets tend to prefer a higher towing point and you will have to make a number of adjustments to suit wind conditions.

fig 9.9

fig 9.10

ROSETTE

I am indebted to Graham Wyle of the Midlands Kite Fliers for the idea of this design, although I must also shamefully admit that it took three attempts before I managed to build one that didn't collapse in mid-air.

The Rosette is basically a high aspect-ratio, hexagonal facet utilising three different colours.

Material	: Rip-stop nylon in 3 colours
Spars	: Ramin dowel. 8 mm ($\frac{5}{16}$ inch) Spine approx 78 cm (31 inches) Bracing spars 6 pieces approx 78 cm (31 inches)
Other materials	: 8 mm ($\frac{5}{16}$ inch) PVC tube split rings 8 × 15 mm ($\frac{5}{8}$ inch) 12 × 12 mm ($\frac{1}{2}$ inch); Slider
Tail	: Tailless
Line	: 35 kg (75 lb)
Wind speed	: Gentle–moderate
Time to make	: 12–15 hrs
Difficulty	: ******

For the central colour you will need three pieces of fabric 52 cm (20$\frac{1}{2}$ inches) × 78 cm (31 inches); for the second colour, six pieces 26 cm (10$\frac{1}{4}$ inches) × 56 cm (22 inches) and six pieces 52 cm (20$\frac{1}{2}$ inches) × 56 cm (22 inches); and for the outer colour twelve pieces 27 cm (10$\frac{1}{2}$ inches) × 26 cm (10$\frac{1}{4}$ inches) and six pieces 52 cm (20$\frac{3}{4}$ inches) × 26 cm (10$\frac{1}{4}$ inches). These pieces must be accurately cut and the sides absolutely parallel. Join them to create the basic shapes using a lapped seam, with a 1 cm ($\frac{3}{8}$ inch) overlap.

Next make the three triangular templates, adding allowances for hemming on two sides only (Fig 9.11).

Fold and crease the fabric pieces along AA^1, BB^1 and CC^1, and cut out the shapes: three large, three-colour diamonds; six intermediate, two-colour diamonds; and six single-colour diamonds. Mark sewing lines very carefully. The rest of the construction follows in a similar way to that for the five-sided facet.

Join the three large diamonds along the (short) diagonal using a narrow length of tape, creating loops at tip and base.

Add the other shapes to create a snowflake pattern: firstly the two-colour diamonds, one to each wing (Fig 9.12); then the six small diamonds (Fig 9.13). Finally, join intermediate wings along the sewing-lines previously drawn (Fig 9.14).

Now sew tape loops to each of the six corner wing-tips and join adjacent wings at the tips in pairs enclosing a short tape loop.

Add suitable connections to the base, tip and to the six corners, then thread 12 mm ($\frac{1}{2}$ inch) split rings to intermediate wing pairs. Next fit the spine and spars carefully, ensuring the sails are evenly tensioned and that there is no more than a slight bow on the bracing spars.

Make a three-leg bridle, each leg approximately 2 metres (7 feet) long, as with previous facets.

Hold your breath until you actually see it fly!

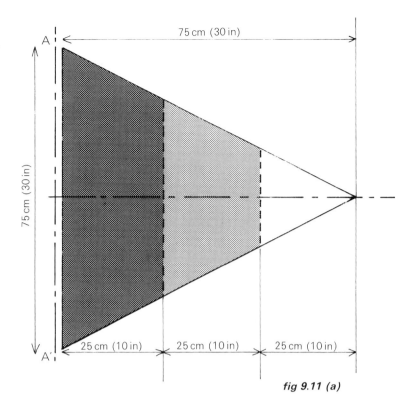

fig 9.11 (a)

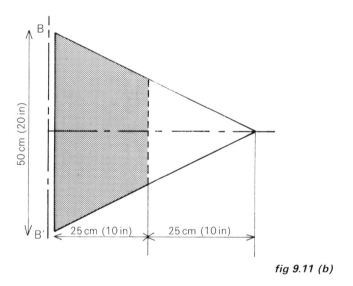

fig 9.11 (b)

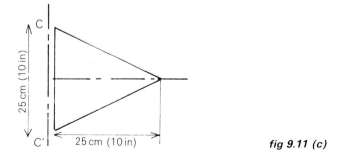

fig 9.11 (c)

87

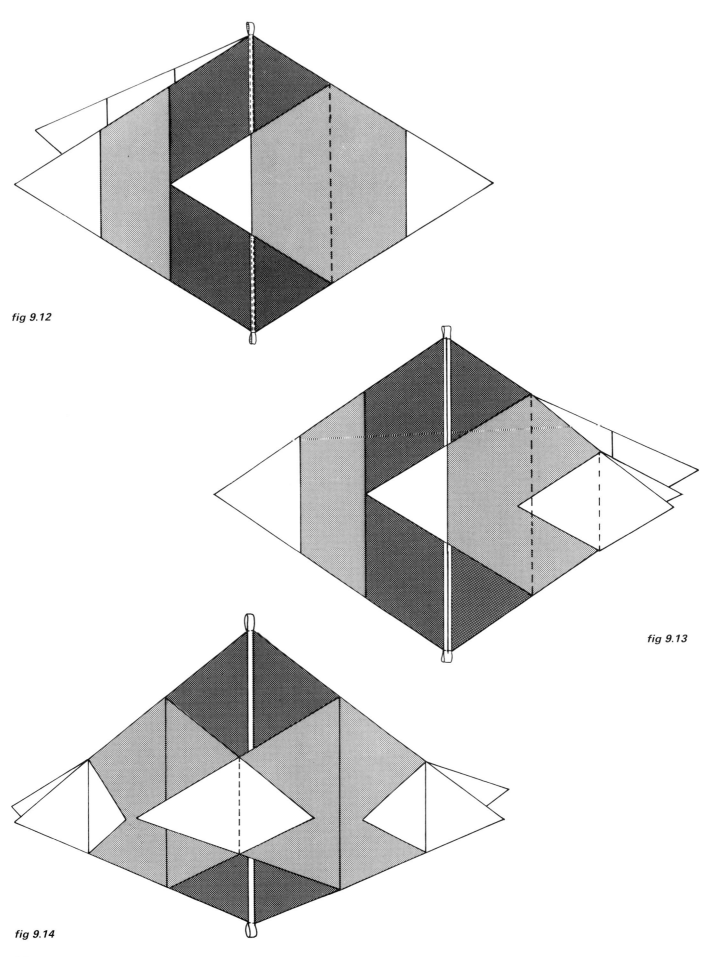

fig 9.12

fig 9.13

fig 9.14

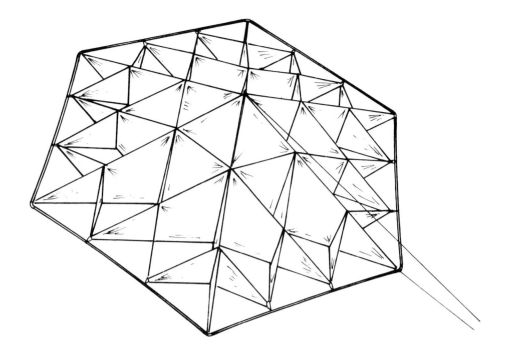

fig 9.15

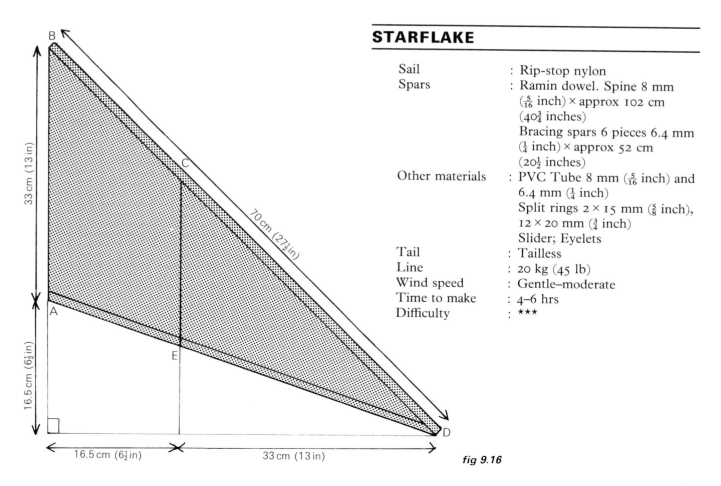

STARFLAKE

Sail	: Rip-stop nylon
Spars	: Ramin dowel. Spine 8 mm ($\frac{5}{16}$ inch) × approx 102 cm (40$\frac{3}{4}$ inches) Bracing spars 6 pieces 6.4 mm ($\frac{1}{4}$ inch) × approx 52 cm (20$\frac{1}{2}$ inches)
Other materials	: PVC Tube 8 mm ($\frac{5}{16}$ inch) and 6.4 mm ($\frac{1}{4}$ inch) Split rings 2 × 15 mm ($\frac{5}{8}$ inch), 12 × 20 mm ($\frac{3}{4}$ inch) Slider; Eyelets
Tail	: Tailless
Line	: 20 kg (45 lb)
Wind speed	: Gentle–moderate
Time to make	: 4–6 hrs
Difficulty	: ★★★

fig 9.16

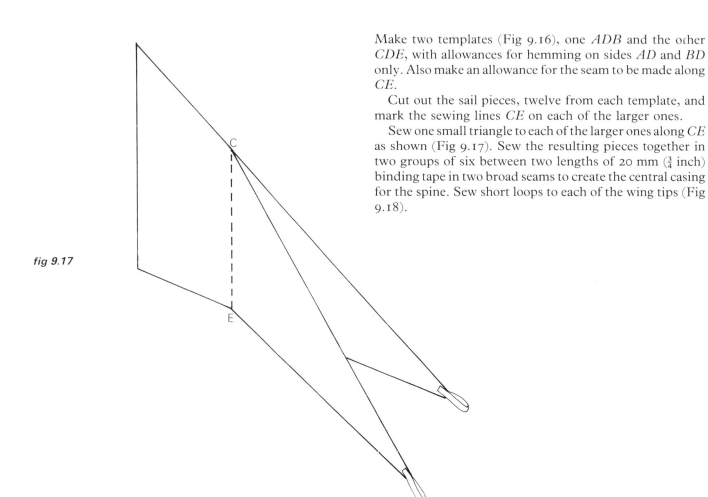

fig 9.17

Make two templates (Fig 9.16), one *ADB* and the other *CDE*, with allowances for hemming on sides *AD* and *BD* only. Also make an allowance for the seam to be made along *CE*.

Cut out the sail pieces, twelve from each template, and mark the sewing lines *CE* on each of the larger ones.

Sew one small triangle to each of the larger ones along *CE* as shown (Fig 9.17). Sew the resulting pieces together in two groups of six between two lengths of 20 mm ($\frac{3}{4}$ inch) binding tape in two broad seams to create the central casing for the spine. Sew short loops to each of the wing tips (Fig 9.18).

fig 9.18

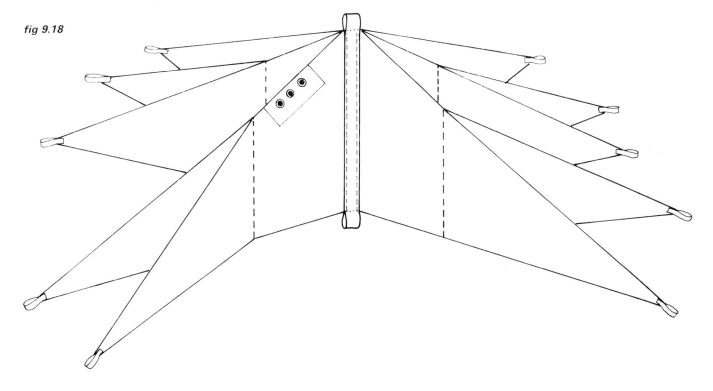

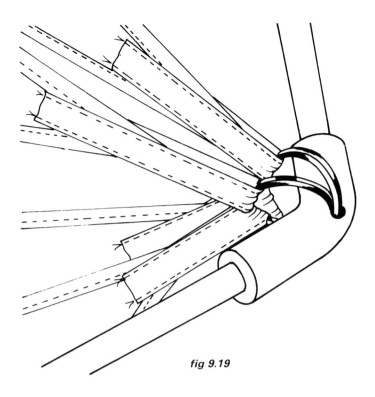

fig 9.19

Reinforce one of the wings with an additional layer of fabric and insert 2–3 eyelets 15–20 cm (6–8 inches) from the tip.

Join the wing tips in groups of four – two upper, two lower – and fit corner tube connections as indicated (Fig 9.19). Add suitable connections at the base and tip. Fit the spine and bracing spars, trimming them so that the sails are tight but evenly tensioned. And finally tie a bracing line along the spine joining the inner loops.

Fit a three-leg bridle from the eyelet to two wing tips as with the facets.

fig 9.20

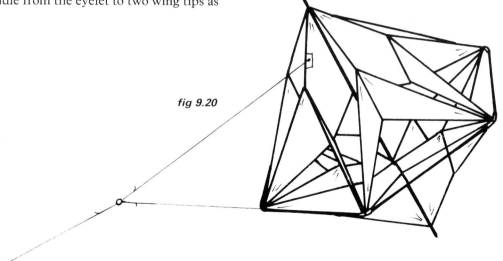

CHAPTER TEN

stunter kites

There can be few kitefliers who claim to take their sport seriously and yet don't have a stunter amongst their collection. When the strong winds blow, away go the sleds, the Eddys and the deltas and out come the stunters; all shapes, all sizes, but all amazingly spectacular.

'Stunter' is the name usually given to a kite having two lines, which can be manoeuvred around the sky under the control of the flier. Pull on the left line and the kite turns in an arc to the left; pull on the right-hand line and it turns to the right; pull evenly on both lines and it lifts. By careful control, the stunter can be made to hover just feet from the ground or dash horizontally across the sky.

Tails on stunters generally slow them down, reducing the speed and manoeuvrability. On the other hand, they can also add just that little bit of drag to assist control, while also bringing colour and excitement to the display.

DELTA WING STUNTER

Sail	: Polythene 300–500 gauge
Spars	: Fibreglass. Spine 6.4 mm ($\frac{1}{4}$ inch) × 107 cm (42$\frac{1}{2}$ inches) Spreader 6.4 mm ($\frac{1}{4}$ inch) tube × 75 cm (30 inches) Leading edge spars 2 pieces 5 mm ($\frac{3}{16}$ inch) × 107 cm (42$\frac{1}{2}$ inches)
Tail	: Tailless
Line	: 2 lines, 25 kg (55 lb) each
Wind speed	: Gentle–moderate
Time to make	: 2–3 hours
Difficulty	: ★★★

The Delta Wing is a fast, powerful, highly-manoeuvreable kite, capable of performing the tightest turns and certainly not one for the weak or faint-hearted.

Cut out the sail according to the template, shown here as a half (Fig 10.1). Score, fold and tape the leading edges to create spar tubes, and reinforce the bridle and spreader attachment points with rip-stop tape.

Connections for the tip and base are shown (Fig 10.2 (a), (b)). Fit the bridle as shown (Fig 10.3). The spreader bar is not fixed at C, but can be held in a loop and should be long enough to create a slight tension in the bracing lines TCT', which of course should be even both sides.

The manoeuvrability of this kite can be altered to suit wind conditions and your flying skill by altering the ratios of lines a, b and c, which for average conditions should be 47 cm (18$\frac{1}{2}$ inches), 44 cm (17$\frac{1}{2}$ inches) and 60 cm (24 inches) respectively.

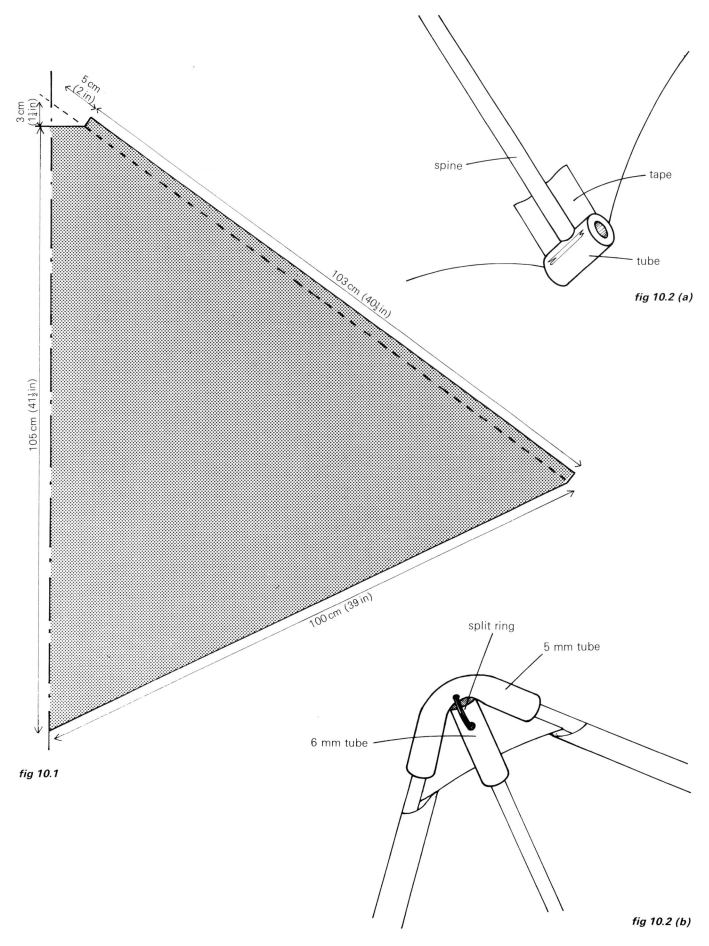

5 cm (2 in)

3 cm (1¼ in)

103 cm (40½ in)

105 cm (41½ in)

100 cm (39 in)

spine

tape

tube

fig 10.2 (a)

fig 10.1

split ring

5 mm tube

6 mm tube

fig 10.2 (b)

93

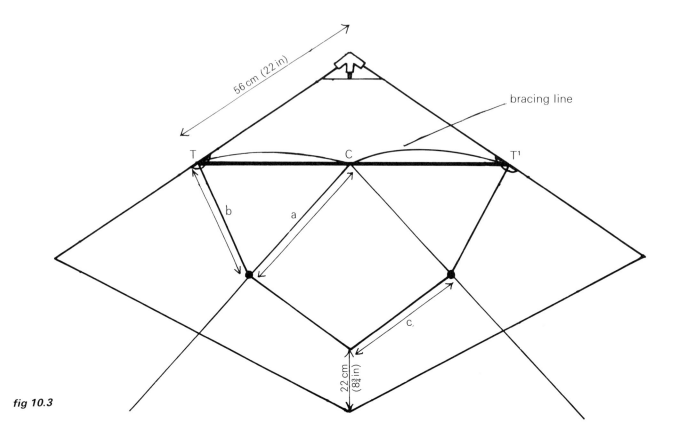

bracing line

T

C

T¹

b

a

c

56 cm (22 in)

22 cm (8¾ in)

fig 10.3

fig 10.4

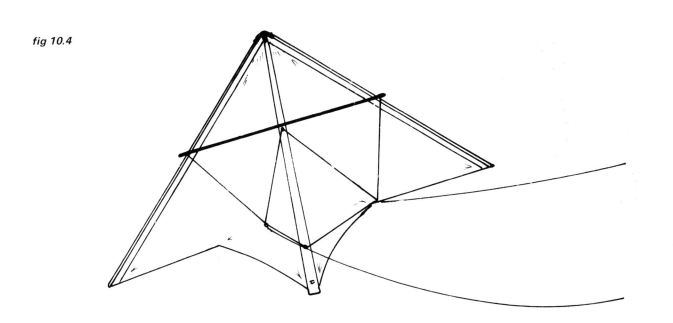

DIAMOND STUNTER

Sail : Rip-stop nylon (spinnaker preferred)

Spars : Fibreglass. Spine 4 mm ($\frac{3}{16}$ inch) × 83 cm (32$\frac{1}{2}$ inches); spar 3 mm ($\frac{1}{8}$ inch) × 82 cm (32$\frac{1}{4}$ inches)

Tail : 10 m (35 feet) ribbon

Line : 2 lines, 15 kg (33 lb) each

Wind speed : Gentle–moderate

Time to make : 2–3 hrs

Difficulty : ★★

Cut out the sail according to the template shown as a half (Fig 10.5). Hem all four edges and make spar connections at tip and base using rip-stop or wide fabric tape and PVC tube as in Fig 10.2 (a). To create the spar pockets sew triangles of fabric, double-folded to the wing tips (Fig 10.6).

Fit the spine just tight, and the cross-spar. The position of the top two bridle points is found by using compasses or dividers set at 22 cm (8$\frac{3}{4}$ inches) and measuring from the tip to the cross-spar. Before making a hole in the sail, however, do make sure that these points are symmetrically placed on either side of the sail. The third bridle point is 13 cm (5 inches) from the base (Fig 10.7). Reinforce the sail at these points and fit eyelets.

Fit the bridles, each 110 cm (44 inches) long tied directly to the spars and spine.

Setting the towing points on the bridles is just a little tricky. They should be low enough for the wind to cause the cross-spar to bow, yet not so low that the kite will not lift. A number of adjustments will need to be made during its maiden flight.

The Diamond should be flown with a long 10-metre (35 feet) tape tail.

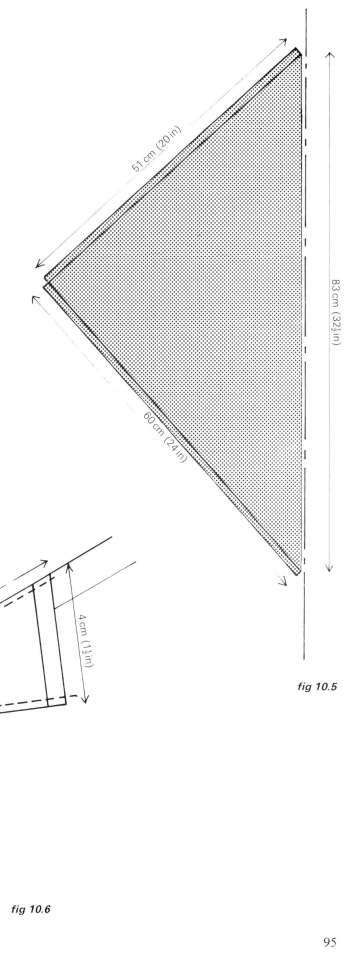

fig 10.5

fig 10.6

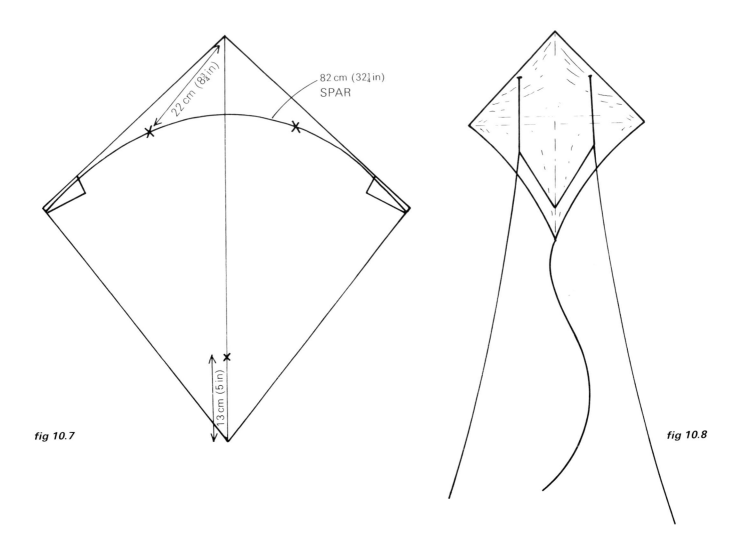

fig 10.7

fig 10.8

STUNTER TRAIN

Here again the basic configuration is a delta, but the sail is a diamond shape rather than a triangle. My own preference is for a stack of five or, if I am feeling very strong, ten.

Sail	: Polythene
Spars	: Fibreglass spine 4 mm ($\frac{5}{32}$ inch) × 71 cm (28 inches) Leading edge spars 2 pieces 3.2 mm ($\frac{1}{8}$ inch) × 47 cm (18$\frac{1}{2}$ inches) Spreaders 3.2 mm ($\frac{1}{8}$ inch) × 36 cm (14$\frac{1}{4}$ inches) Control bar 8 mm ($\frac{5}{16}$ inch) × 38 cm (15 inches)
Additional materials	: PVC tube 3.2 mm ($\frac{1}{8}$ inch)
Line	: 10 stack 2 lines 50 kg (100 lb)
Tail	: None
Wind speeds	: Gentle–fresh
Time to make	: Each kite 15–30 mins plus 3–4 hrs to bridle stack
Difficulty	: ★★★

Cut out the sails according to the template, shown here as a half (Fig 10.9).

Crease, fold and tape a narrow strip along the leading edge to create tight tubes for the spars. Reinforce the trailing edges.

The spreader bar will be jointed directly to the leading edge spars, rather than to the sail as in previous designs, and suitable PVC connections should be made as described in Chapter 4. The tip joint can be made by threading a short length of 3 mm tube through a hole at one end of the 4 mm (spine) tube (Fig 10.10). Use a base connection as in Fig 10.2.

Fit the spars, spines and spreaders. When fitting the spreaders it is useful to have a glue gun handy. Squirt some molten glue into the tubes and force the fibreglass rod in quickly afterwards, ensuring a good tight joint. Do the same at the tip.

The stack is jointed at four points *PQRS*, kites 90 cm (36 inches) apart. Reinforce the sail at these points using rip-stop tape. (Fig 10.11).

The control bar is fitted as shown, including suggested dimensions for the bridles (Fig 10.12). To adjust the

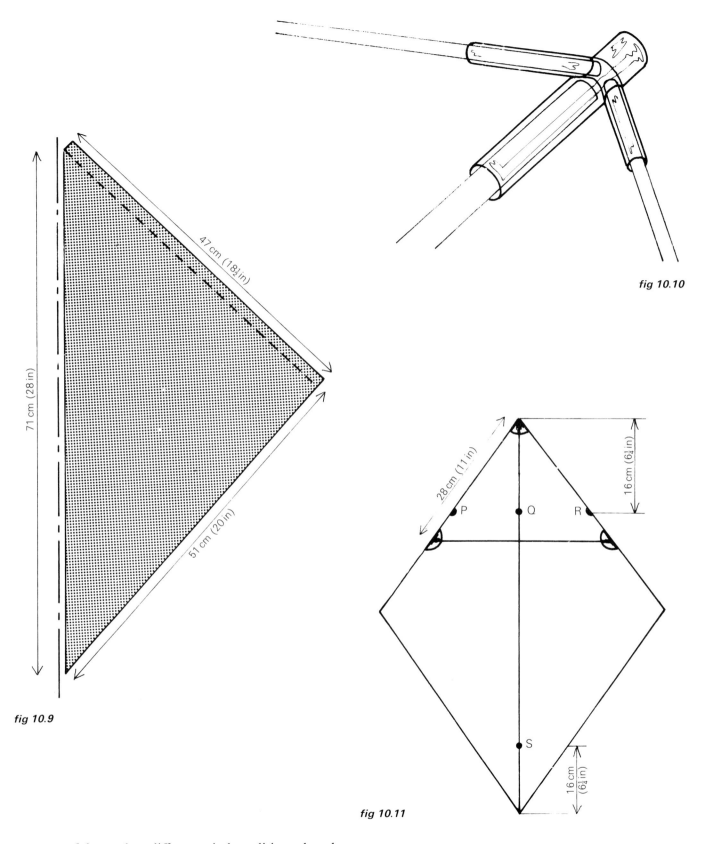

47 cm (18½ in)

71 cm (28 in)

51 cm (20 in)

fig 10.9

fig 10.10

28 cm (11 in)

16 cm (6¼ in)

P Q R

S

16 cm (6¼ in)

fig 10.11

response of the stack to different wind conditions alter the ratio of lines *a*, *b* and *c*.

When attempting to launch a stack of three or more you will need the help of an assistant. Take hold of the lines, tensioning them slightly, while the assistant holds the tail kite, and as the tension increases haul the kites into the air.

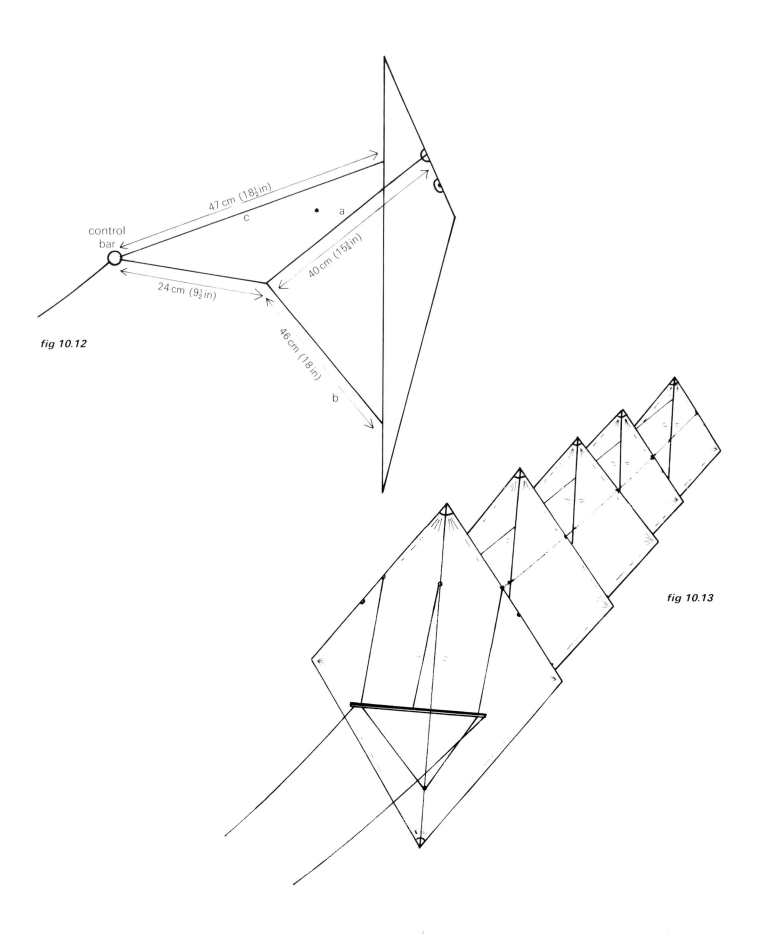

47 cm (18½ in)

c

a

control
bar

40 cm (15¾ in)

24 cm (9½ in)

46 cm (18 in)

b

fig 10.12

fig 10.13

CHAPTER ELEVEN

sleds

It is easy to be fooled by the sled into assessing its qualities purely by its ease of construction. But with imagination, flair and just a little skill the simple sled can match the beauty and grace of any other design.

MINI SLED

Quite recently I attended a festival in Lancashire. The wind was howling across the field and nothing would fly – well at least, not in the view of the 'experts'. While most of us had forsaken our kites for hot coffee and sandwiches, a group of young boys decided to fly their sleds made at a workshop the previous week. So much for the experts! This was what they were flying.

Sail	:	Tyvek, wrapping paper, newspaper
Spars	:	30 cm (12 inches) Bamboo kebab skewers
Line	:	2–3 kg (4–6 lb)
Tail	:	Ribbon 1 cm ($\frac{3}{8}$ inch) × 1.5 m (5 feet)
Time to make	:	10–15 mins
Difficulty	:	★

Make up the template as in Fig 11.1. Fold the sail material, lay the template along the fold and cut out the shape. Next tape the skewers in place. Tape small rings at the towing points and finally add the tails and bridle, 120 cm (48 inches) looped at the centre (Fig 11.2).

What else is there to do except to fly it?

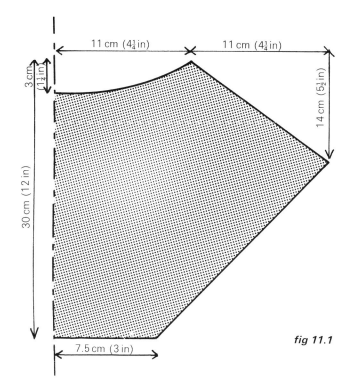

fig 11.1

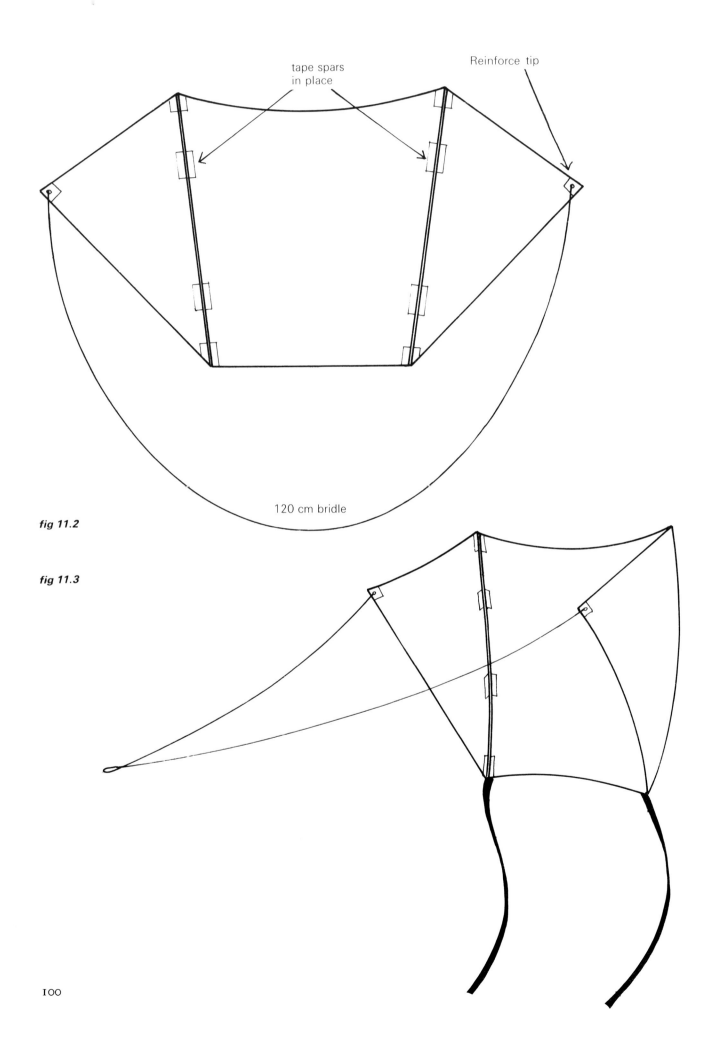

tape spars
in place

Reinforce tip

120 cm bridle

fig 11.2

fig 11.3

GRAUEL SLED

This sled, one of the many developed by Ed Grauel, makes use of two vents in the lower half of the sail to create additional stability.

Sail	: Polythene, Tyvek
Spars	: 5 mm ($\frac{3}{16}$ inch) dowel 2 pieces 60.5 cm (24 inches)
Line	: 7 kg (15 lb)
Tail	: Tailless
Wind speed	: Light–gentle
Time to make	: 30–45 mins
Difficulty	: ★

The template is shown as a sail half (Fig 11.4). Position the centre line along a fold in the polythene and cut around through two layers. This will ensure symmetry. Reinforce the edges with tape. The outer wing-tips should be further reinforced with rip-stop tape and punched to accept the bridle (Fig 11.5).

The bridle should be 2 metres (7 feet) long with a loop at the centre.

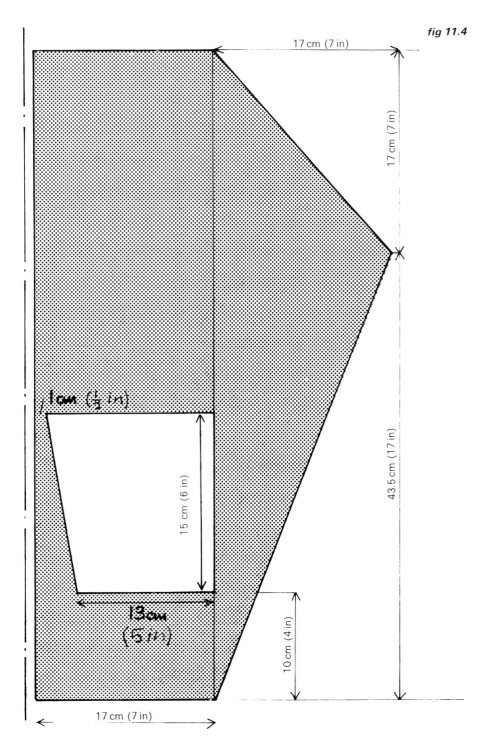

fig 11.4

17 cm (7 in)

17 cm (7 in)

43.5 cm (17 in)

1 cm ($\frac{1}{2}$ in)

15 cm (6 in)

13 cm (5 in)

10 cm (4 in)

17 cm (7 in)

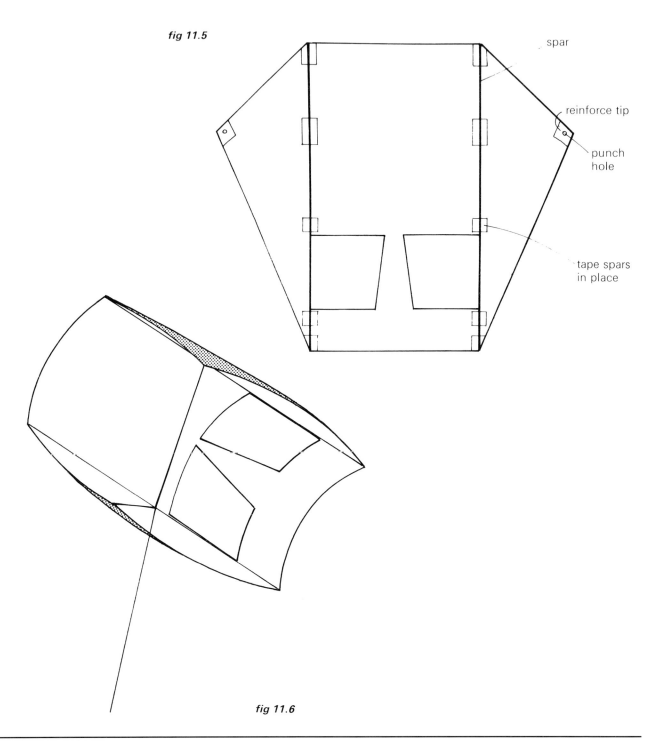

fig 11.5

spar

reinforce tip

punch hole

tape spars in place

fig 11.6

BULLET SLED

Sail	:	Polythene, Tyvek, wrapping paper
Spars	:	Dowel 5 mm ($\frac{3}{16}$ inch) 3 pieces 66 cm (24 inches)
Line	:	7 kg (15 lb)
Tail	:	Tape 1 cm ($\frac{3}{8}$ inch) × 1.5 m (5 feet)
Wind speeds	:	Light–moderate
Time to make	:	1–2 hrs
Difficulty	:	★★

Ed Grauel's original construction has been adapted to require just a single template (Fig 11.7). Cut out two pieces of sail this shape.

Fold each sail piece along CD and tape them together along this line. Now bring edges AB across to EF and tape them in place, creating a tube on each side. Next tape the spars to the reverse of the kite along AB and CD. Reinforce the towing points with rip-stop tape and punch holes to accept the bridle (Fig 11.8).

Ed suggests a bridle of 4 metres (13 feet) with a loop at the centre. A streamer tail or drogue can be attached to the midpoint of the trailing edges if necessary.

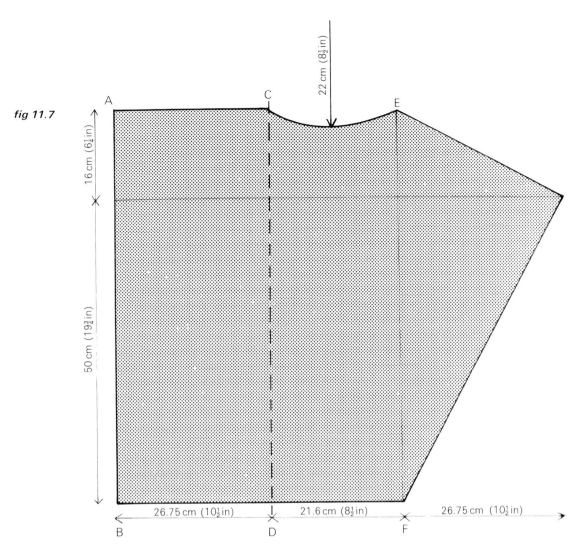

fig 11.7

22 cm (8½in)

A   C   E

16 cm (6¼in)

50 cm (19¾in)

26.75 cm (10½in)   21.6 cm (8½in)   26.75 cm (10½in)

B   D   F

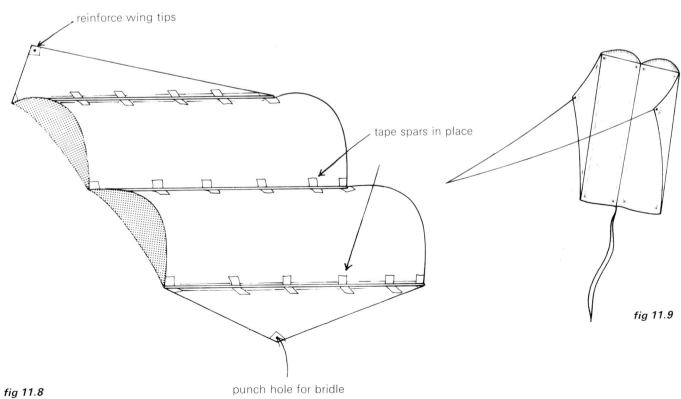

reinforce wing tips

tape spars in place

fig 11.9

fig 11.8

punch hole for bridle

POCKET SLED

Sail	:	Polythene, Tyvek, wrapping paper, newspaper
Spars	:	None
Line	:	7 kg (15 lb)
Tail	:	None
Wind speeds	:	Light–gentle
Time to make	:	30–45 mins
Difficulty	:	★

fig 11.10 (a)

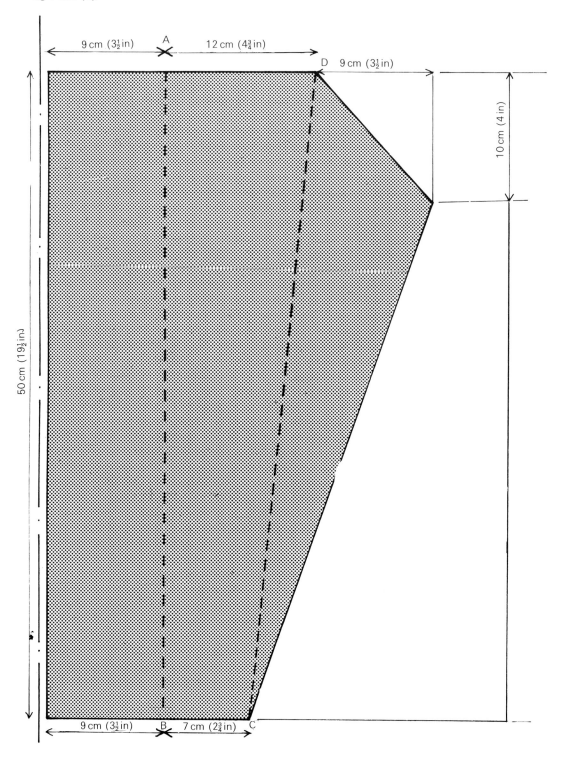

9 cm (3½ in)   A   12 cm (4¾ in)   D   9 cm (3½ in)

10 cm (4 in)

50 cm (19½ in)

9 cm (3½ in)   B   7 cm (2¾ in)   C

Make two templates (Fig 11.10 (a) and (b)). Lay the centre-line of the larger template along a fold in the sail material and cut two symmetrical halves. Cut out two additional pieces of material to make the stabilising tubes: template 11.10 (b).

Tape the smaller shapes along lines *AB* and *CD* on the sail, making sure that they are fitted the correct way round. Next tape small rings to the outer tips to accept the bridle or reinforce and punch as with previous sleds. Tie the 3-metre (13 feet) bridle to each corner and make a loop at its centre to take the flying line.

In turbulent conditions the pocket sled will require a tail or drogue attached to the mid point of the trailing edge.

One final point: to store this kite, roll rather than fold it, as if the stabilising tubes become creased it will become difficult, if not impossible, to fly.

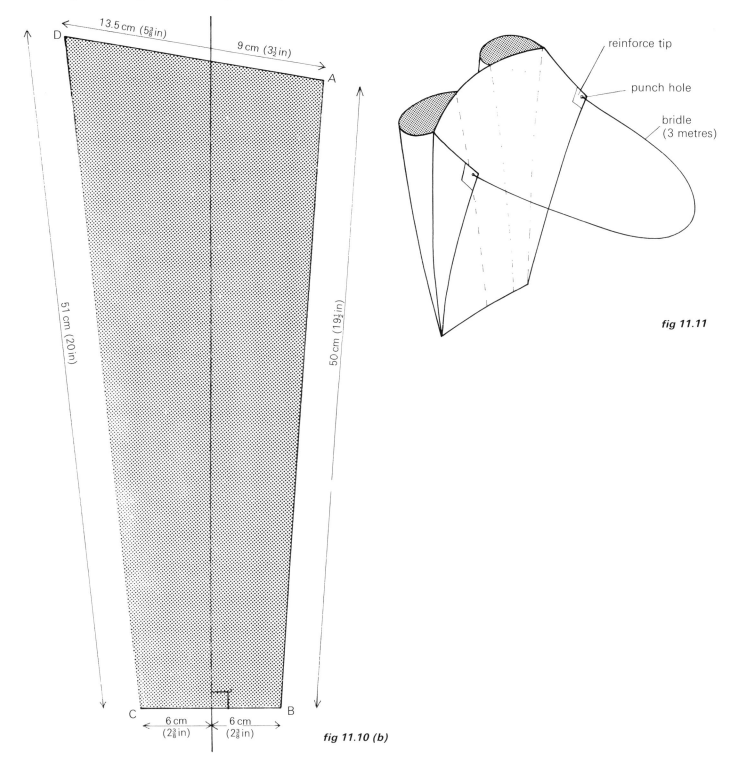

fig 11.10 (b)

fig 11.11

CHAPTER TWELVE

parafoils

I have to admit that I am not a great lover of parafoils, as even little ones seem sluggish and unresponsive, although with skill they can be made very attractive and are of course very powerful lifters.

Parafoil I is relatively simple to make, but its performance is adequate rather than outstanding; Parafoil II is a much larger version, again with quite acceptable qualities. The Flowform, on the other hand, is a novel design, using slightly different principles of flight, and is marginally easier to make.

PARAFOIL DESIGN

The most common aerofoil section used with parafoils is the Clark Y with the section depth of 18% of the chord, occurring at a point 30% from the leading edge. To create the aerofoil section, draw a line to the length of the required chord and divide it into 100 units. Graph paper is very useful here. Mark points vertically as indicated in Table 12.1, but do remember that these are percentages of the chord, not absolute values.

For maximum performance the air inlet on the leading edge should be as shallow as possible, but if it is too small, the parafoil will not fill effectively. Values of 8–12% are common. Similarly in relation to inlet depth 5–10% are typical values (Fig 12.1).

Where parafoil designers show their skill and individuality is in relation to the size, shape and relative position of the ventrals, or fins, which can make the difference between a design stable in almost any wind and one which continually wanders about the sky. I have seen lots of complicated mathematics describing values of ventral sizes, etc., but really the only sure way is by trial and error.

Shrouding, too, is particularly awkward and should be worked out by scale drawing. The purpose of the shrouds is to hold the kite in shape into the wind and they, like the ventrals, play an important part in kite performance. Draw a line to scale, the span of your parafoil, and divide it up equally according to the number of cells (Fig 12.2). Draw a perpendicular line at the centre, typically 0.6 to 0.8 times the span, and join lines drawn from each cell to this point. Subtract the width of the ventral from the total length of the line and you have the individual shroud lengths.

Tie each shroud in place and measure it off according to the scale. It is probably easier to work from a loop at the towing point towards the kite. At the towing point end gather the loops on each set of shrouds into a single line, and tie all of them together to create a satisfactory flying angle. It sounds complicated, but the idea comes over a little better in the illustration.

On the kite's maiden flight, individual shrouds/lines may have to be altered marginally to improve stability or shape.

Table 12.1 Aerofoil shape
This shape has been used on both Parafoil 1 and II

Distance from leading edge (% of chord)	Height of aerofoil section (% of chord length)
0	11 (inlet height)
2.5	12.25
5	13.5
10	15.5
15	16.75
20	17.2
30	18
40	17.5
50	16
60	14
70	11.5
80	8
90	4.25
100	0

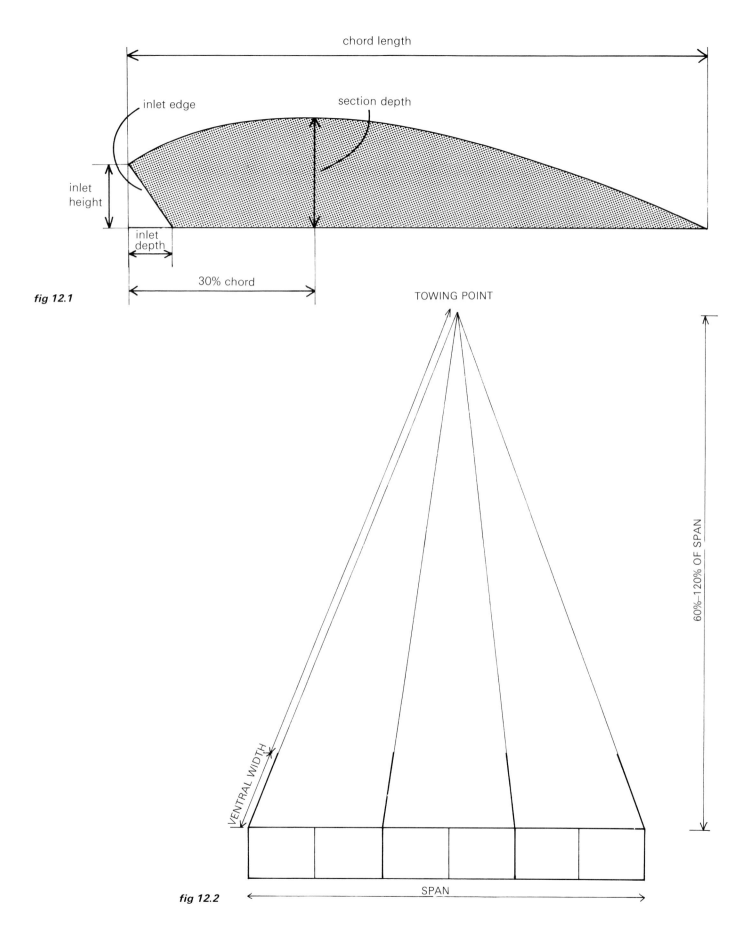

chord length

inlet edge

section depth

inlet
height

inlet
depth

30% chord

fig 12.1

TOWING POINT

60%–120% OF SPAN

VENTRAL WIDTH

fig 12.2

SPAN

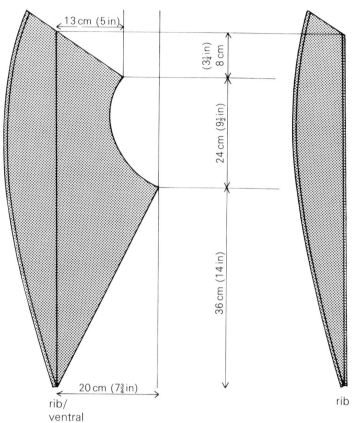

rib/
ventral

fig 12.3

rib

PARAFOIL I

Sail	: Rip-stop nylon
Spars	: None
Tail	: Ribbon tail or drogue
Line	: 30 kg (65 lb)
Wind speeds	: Light–moderate
Time to make	: 4–6 hrs
Difficulty	: ★★★

For this particular design I have used a chord length of 76 cm (30 inches). A unit is thus 7.6 mm ($\frac{3}{10}$ inch). Inlet height 11%; inlet depth 10%.

Cut out the three rib sections, four ventral sections, three cell fronts and the back according to the templates (Figs 12.3, 12.4). It is probably better to edge-bind the pieces rather than hem. Mark sewing-lines on all pieces as indicated.

Sew one of the rib pieces to the rear of each cell front, then join them together enclosing the ventral sections (Fig 12.5 (a), (b)). Sew the inner ribs to the back along the sewing lines. The outer ventral sections should be sewn as indicated in Fig 12.6, thus producing a neater finish.

Fold the trailing edge to sew a narrow hem. Fit tape ties to the corners of the fins and to the centre of the trailing edge, to accept the drogue line.

Shroud according to standard instructions above.

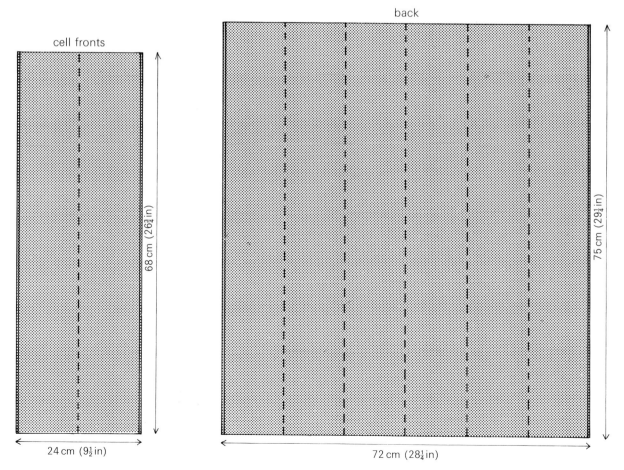

cell fronts

back

fig 12.4

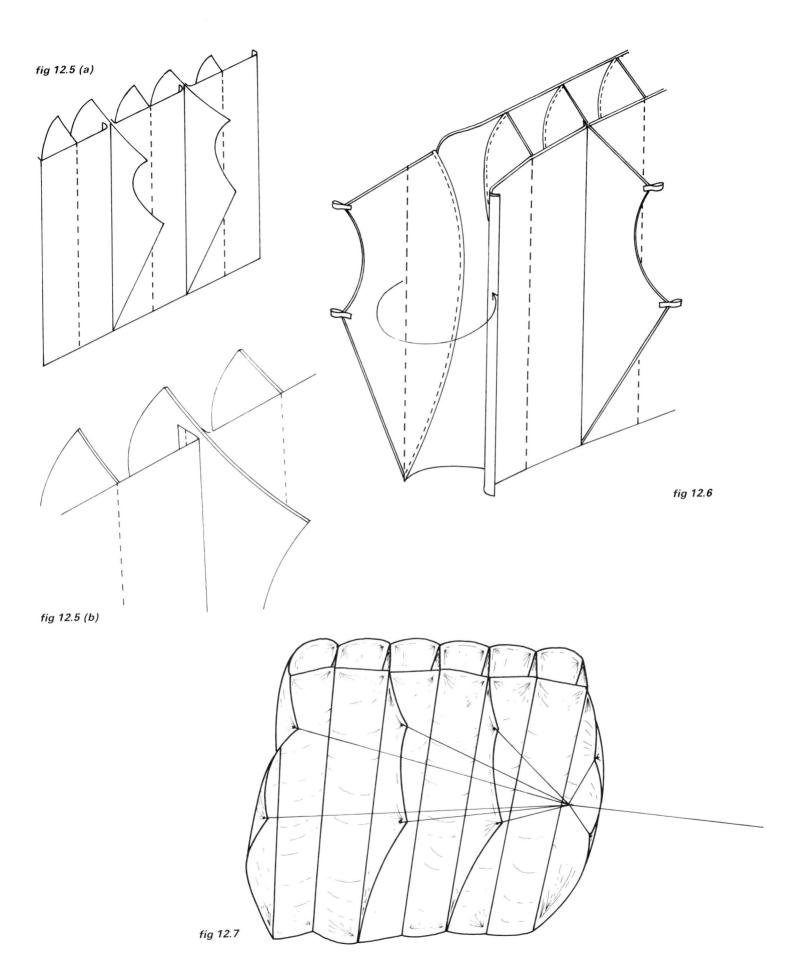

fig 12.5 (a)

fig 12.5 (b)

fig 12.6

fig 12.7

PARAFOIL II

The principles of design and construction established with Parafoil I can be utilised with a much larger design. Here the chord length is 86 cm (34 inches) aspect ratio 1.5 with 8 cells, each 20 cm (8 inches) wide.

fig 12.9

Sail	:	Rip-stop nylon
Spars	:	None
Tail	:	Drogue
Line	:	35 kg (75 lb)
Wind speed	:	Light–moderate
Time to make	:	6–8 hrs
Difficulty	:	★★★★

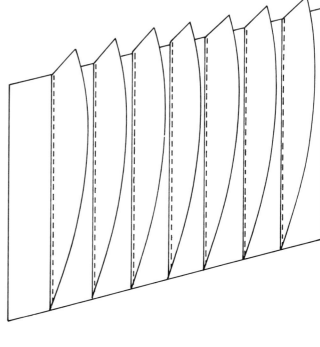

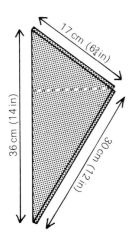

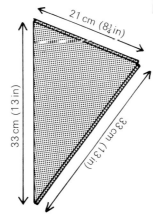

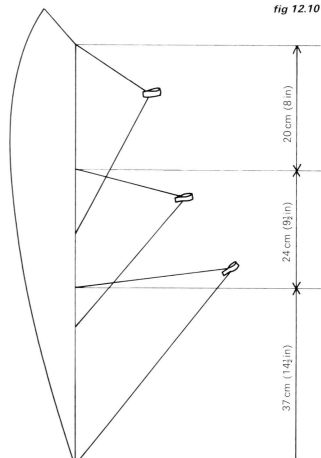

fig 12.10

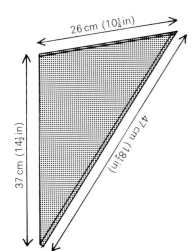

fig 12.8

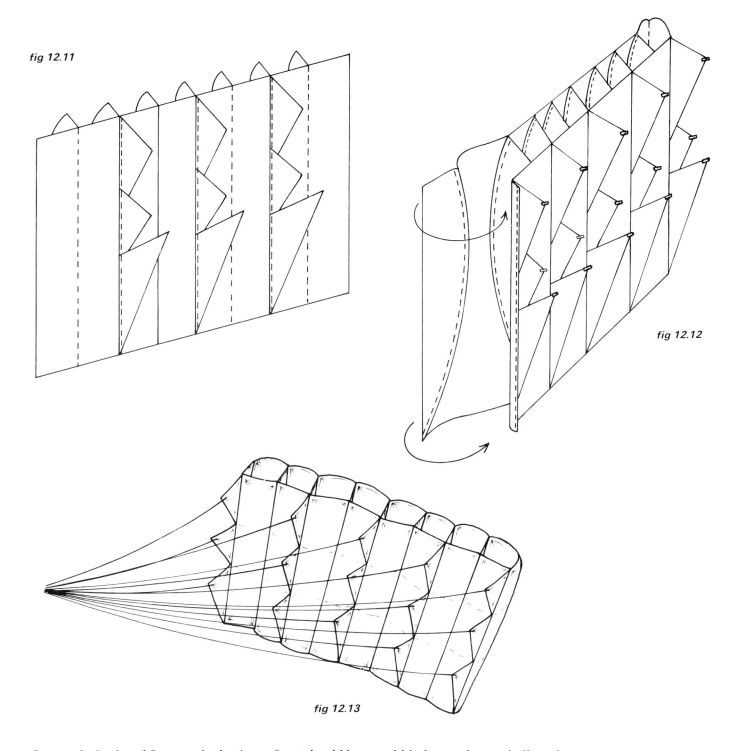

fig 12.11

fig 12.12

fig 12.13

Cut out the back and front as single pieces: front should be 83 cm (32½ inches) × 121 cm (47½ inches), the back will work out at 95 cm (37½ inches) × 121 cm (47½ inches). Within these dimensions there are allowances for seams at the sides and the fold at the trailing edge.

Bind one of the longer sides of each piece and mark rib sewing lines.

Draw your aerofoil template from the table above making allowance for seams on the upper and lower edges. For this design I have used an 11% inlet height and 6% inlet depth. Cut out 5 ribs and bind the inlet edge.

Cut out 5 ventrals from each of the templates in Fig 12.8

and bind two edges as indicated.

Sew the inner ribs to the rear of the front piece along the lines previously drawn (Fig 12.9). Then, using the pattern in Fig 12.10, sew all five sets of ventrals in place as in Fig 12.11.

Now sew the inner ribs to the back starting from one side. Finally sew the outside ribs, folded inwards then sewn to the front and ventral. This method of construction is a little awkward but does ensure a neater finish to the kite (Fig 12.12).

Sew short tape loops to the ventral tips and shroud according to instructions as above.

SUTTON FLOWFORM

The 'Flowform' was originally developed as a competition parachute by Steven Sutton and only later redesigned as a kite. 'Flowform' is a registered trade mark and the design protected by numerous patents throughout the world. It is published here with permission of Steven Sutton.

Sail	: Spinnaker rip-stop
Spars	: None
Line	: 20 kg (40 lb)
Tail	: None
Wind speed	: Light–fresh
Time to make	: 4–6 hrs
Difficulty	: ★★★

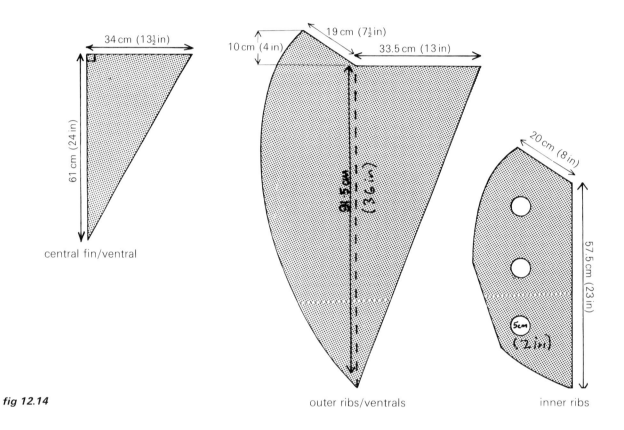

fig 12.14

central fin/ventral

outer ribs/ventrals

inner ribs

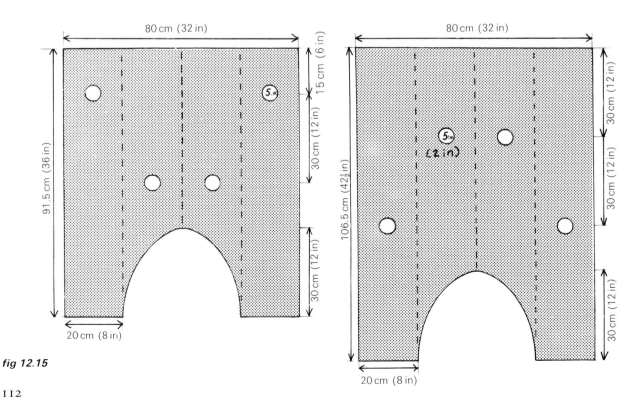

fig 12.15

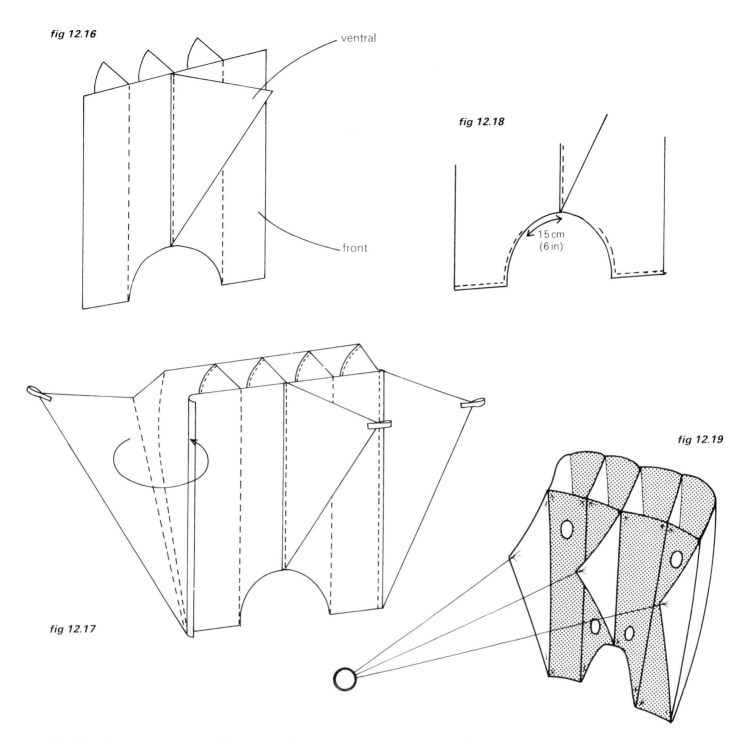

fig 12.16

ventral

front

fig 12.18

15 cm
(6 in)

fig 12.17

fig 12.19

The Flowform uses a slightly different aerofoil section from the previous designs. It is on the whole much squatter, having a section depth of 33%, occurring at 33% of the chord, inlet height of 15% and inlet depth 10%.

The design illustrated here uses a chord length of 101.5 cm (40½ inches), in which case the dimensions translate to: section depth 33.5 cm (13 inches) at 33.5 cm (13 inches); inlet height 15.25 cm (6 inches) and inlet depth 10.1 cm (4 inches).

Cut out the front, back and rib sections as illustrated (Figs 12.14, 12.15). The central rib shapes follow roughly that of the aerofoil section, and again this design is probably better edge-bound than hemmed.

Sew the ribs and centre fin to the front surface of the kite as shown (Fig 12.16), and sew the two outer ventrals to the back. Now working from one side stitch the whole shape together (Fig 12.17).

At the trailing edge sew the front and back together in a flat seam but leave a gap of 15 cm (6 inches) each side across the top of the arch (Fig 12.18).

Sew small loops at the tips of each ventral.

The Flowform is fitted with extremely long shrouds, typically 3 m (10 feet).

This version reproduced with acknowledgement to Margaret Greger from *Kites for Everyone*.

rotor kites

Although they are attractive and fun to fly, rotors are usually quite fragile and extremely difficult to transport – put two or three in a car boot and it's full. But one at least deserves a place in every kiteflier's collection.

If you're used to flying conventional kites, then rotors will seem awkward. They're not as easy to launch and don't respond in quite the same way to line control, but on the other hand they can be interesting to fly and made very colourful.

The direction of spin should always be such that the top is moving away from you.

SINGLE STABILISER

Sail	:	6 mm (¼ inch) polystyrene
Spar	:	Ramin square section moulding 6.4 mm (¼ inch) × 81 cm (32 inches)
Other materials	:	2 bolts or pins 3 mm (⅛ inch) diameter 3–4 cm (1 inch) long 2 flat plastic strips/rods 3 cm (1 inch) long
Line	:	7 kg (15 lb)
Wind	:	Light–gentle
Time to make	:	1–2 hrs
Difficulty	:	**

Cut the rod square at each end and lightly sand along its length. Drill a 3 mm (⅛ inch) diameter hole to a depth of 2.5 cm (1 inch) along the axis of the rod at each end. Next drill holes in each end of the plastic strips, then thread the bolts through one of these holes and glue them into the ends of the rod (Fig 13.1).

Cut out two semi-elliptical shapes of polystyrene as shown (Fig 13.2), and glue or tape them each side of the wooden rod. Since this central joint will take a lot of strain, the adhesive is probably best left overnight to set. Cut out the stabilising circle of polystyrene together with the narrow *S* slit as shown (Fig 13.3).

Thread the ellipse through the *S* section so that both

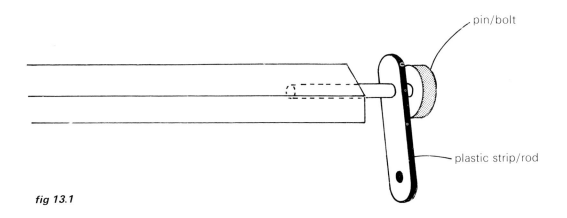

fig 13.1

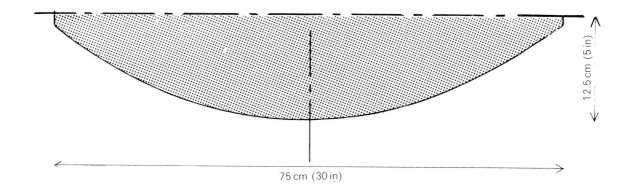

fig 13.2

12.5 cm (5 in)

75 cm (30 in)

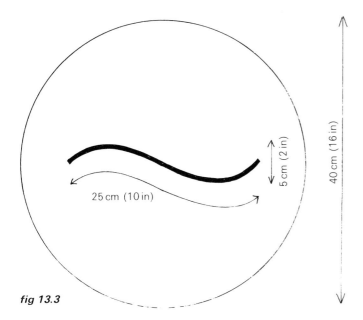

fig 13.3

25 cm (10 in)

5 cm (2 in)

40 cm (16 in)

sides are symmetrical and glue them in position. You may have to shape the wing into the *S* section before inserting it. Use a hairdryer to slightly soften, but not melt, the polystyrene.

Finally, tie a long 4 m (9 feet) bridle to the second holes in the plastic rods with a loop at the centre, allowing the kite to spin freely.

In the illustrations I have included dimensions for a kite which I have found flies well, but this design can of course be scaled up or down, or the shape of the elliptical wing altered. The only criterion seems to be that the area of the stabilising circle should be about two thirds that of the elliptical wing. It is also possible to fit two stabilising discs, one at each end.

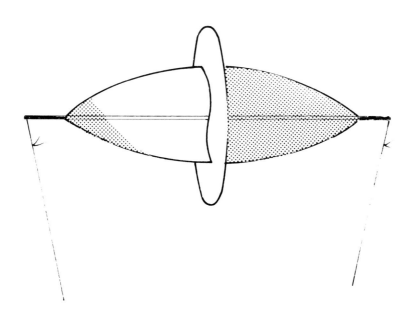

fig 13.4

TWIN 'H'-FORM ROTOR

This rotor is slightly easier to launch than the single stabiliser above, and flies at a marginally higher angle, but on the other hand is not quite as stable.

Sail	: 6 mm ($\frac{1}{4}$ inch) polystyrene
Spars	: 3 mm ($\frac{1}{8}$ inch) Fibreglass 65 cm (26 inches)
Other materials	: High-density plastic or fibreglass tube 3 cm ($1\frac{1}{4}$ inches) long
Line	: 7 kg (15 lb)
Wind speeds	: Light–gentle
Time to make	: 2–3 hrs
Difficulty	: ★★

Cut out two wings and four discs as shown in Fig 13.5 and mark the centre line, axis of rotation, on each wing. Bend each of them into an *S* shape using a hairdryer as described above, but do be very careful to get the curves even over both sides.

Glue discs to each end of the wings, making sure that they are perpendicular and reinforce the centre by glueing a small circle of flat plastic or cardboard, about 4 cm ($1\frac{3}{4}$ inches) diameter, in position (Fig 13.6).

Thread the fibreglass rod through the centres of the stabilising discs, and tape it in place along the wing axes previously drawn. At the centre, the junction of the two rotors, you should also thread the small plastic tube to create a simple bearing around which the kite can rotate.

The flying line is attached to this central plastic tube.

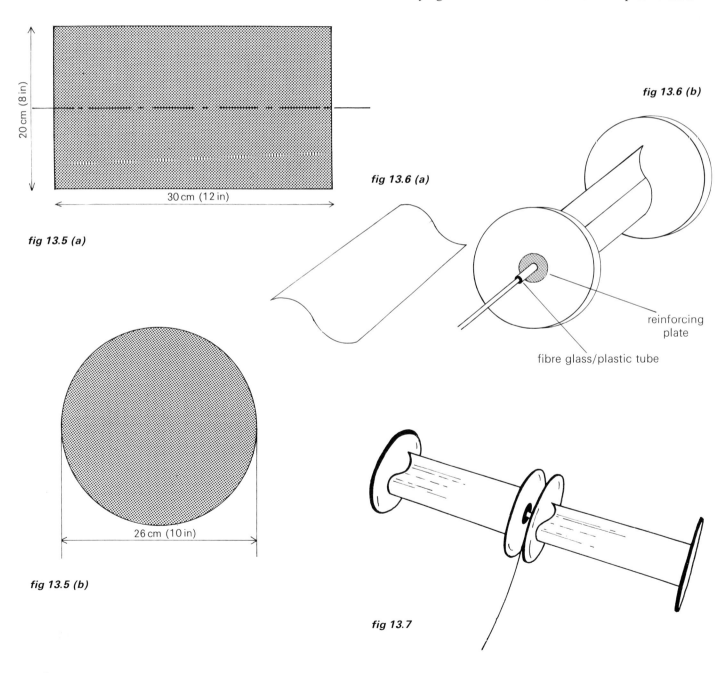

20 cm (8 in)

30 cm (12 in)

fig 13.5 (a)

26 cm (10 in)

fig 13.5 (b)

fig 13.6 (b)

fig 13.6 (a)

reinforcing plate

fibre glass/plastic tube

fig 13.7

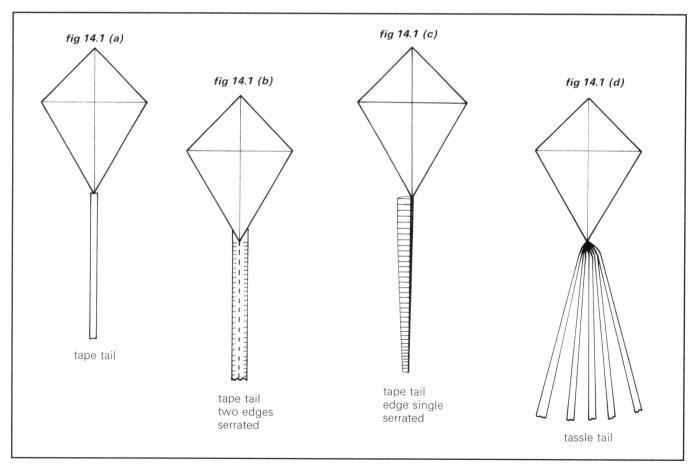

C|HAPTER FOURTEEN

tails

Whether a kite should or should not have a tail is an argument that has occupied the attention of a good many kite designers, and none has reached any significant conclusion.

On the one hand, the modern kitemaker seeks to make an aerodynamically efficient kite that does not require a tail for stability. But equally, a tail can add colour, shape, form and dignity to an otherwise boring, shapeless and undignified kite, and we would be foolish to deprive it of such qualities just for the sake of pride.

Tape/ribbon tails
The simplest form of tail can be made by fixing strips of rip-stop, PVC or polythene to the trailing edge of the kite. Neat and effective (Fig 14.1 (a)).

To enhance the effect of the tape tail, both in terms of colour and aerodynamics, two or three layers of material can be joined and the edges serrated (Fig 14.1 (b), (c)).

Tassle/donkey tails
Here strips of fabric or polythene are collected and tied together, and fixed either at the base of the kite, or at the end of a single tape tail (Fig 14.1 (d)).

fig 14.1 (a)

fig 14.1 (b)

fig 14.1 (c)

fig 14.1 (d)

tape tail

tape tail
two edges
serrated

tape tail
edge single
serrated

tassle tail

Loop tails

Where a kite has a suitable trailing edge, a long tape tail can be attached to either end, creating a loop – quite effective despite its simplicity. An enhancement of this is of course the ladder tail, made of multiple loops, although these are now regarded as somewhat old-fashioned (Fig 14.1 (e)).

Flat tails

Serpent kites, and sometimes hexagon kites, usually feature flat tails, but have you ever seen what a beautiful, flat tail can do for a sled or a parafoil. Try it!

The width of the top of the tail is usually made the same as that of the kite's trailing edge, slowly tapering and supported via a rod and two lines, at a distance equal to the length of the trailing edge away from it (Fig 14.1 (f)).

Flat tails are made from wide sections of sail material, and can be decorated by appliqué, embroidery or any simple combination of colours.

Tubular tails

These can be made from tubes of fabric 6–8 cm (2–3 inches) in diameter or, more usually, coloured polythene. They are most often used on stunters, but can of course be fitted to almost any kite.

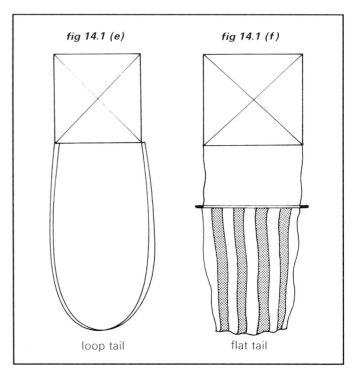

fig 14.1 (e)   *fig 14.1 (f)*

loop tail   flat tail

DROGUES

A drogue is a cup-shaped, drag-inducing device which, when attached to the trailing edge of a kite, can have a substantial stabilising effect.

As a very rough guide, the diameter of the larger end of the drogue should be between one tenth and one fifth of the length of the kite's trailing edge. For example, a parafoil with a one-metre trailing edge would require a drogue of 10–20 cm diameter. Much, however, depends on the kite's inherent stability.

Standard drogue

There are numerous designs of drogue published, but I have found this one to be the most efficient. The dimensions should be regarded as ratios rather than absolute.

Cut out four pieces of fabric as shown and join them along *AB* to create a cone (Fig 14.2). Bind the edges of both open ends. Next sew tape loops to the middle of each section and tie a short line to each. Gather the lines together evenly so that each is a cone diameter in length, and make an overhand loop, which is then attached to the trailing edge of the kite via a long line and 2–3 swivels in series (Fig 14.3).

As with a standard tail, the longer the drogue line the greater the stabilising effect.

Spinning drogue

The drogue can be used not only to stabilise the kite but also to enhance the display by making it spin. The simplest method of making the drogue turn is of course to cut asymmetrical holes in the sections of the standard shape (Fig 14.4).

A more spectacular effect can, however, be created by a spinning device such as that illustrated, although this design is perhaps more for decoration than stability.

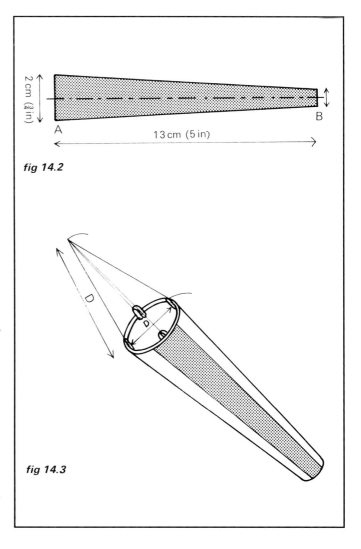

2 cm (¾ in)

A   B

13 cm (5 in)

fig 14.2

D

D

fig 14.3

Cut out six triangles of fabric as shown. Since these pieces are not going to be hemmed, hot cutting is preferable (Fig 14.5).

Bind the pieces together to create a hoop as shown. I have found that the spinner is slightly more effective if you include some stiffening (interlining) with the binding.

Join the pieces at the centre, using a small circle of fabric. Sew six small ties at the centres of the edges *AB* and tie lines

20 cm (8 inches) long. Join the lines so that the drogue is balanced, and make a loop. Tie the drogue to your kite using 2–3 swivels in series (Fig 14.6).

The effect of this drogue can be further enhanced if combined in pairs along the kite's trailing edge, so that these spin in opposite directions. Streamers can also be attached.

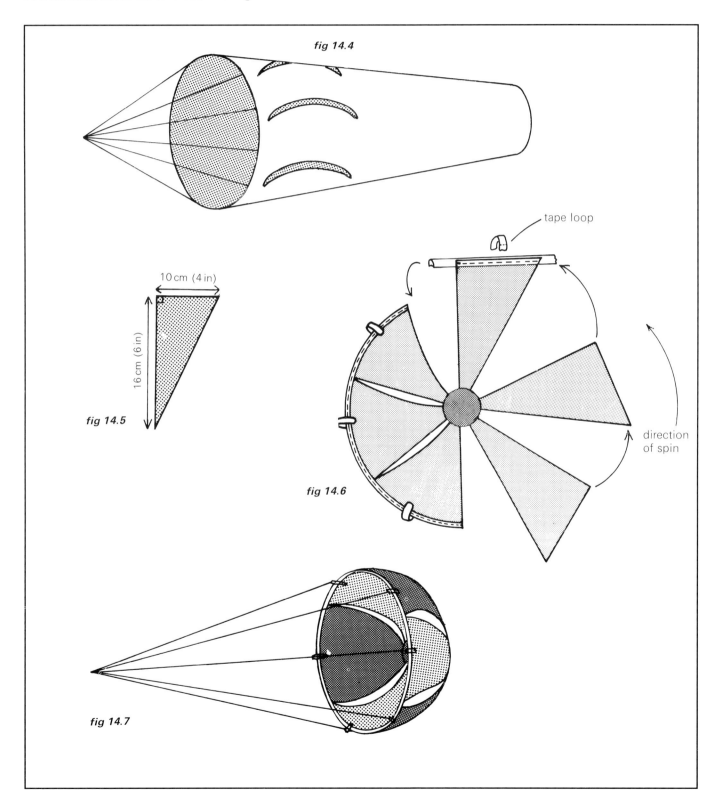

fig 14.4

10 cm (4 in)

16 cm (6 in)

fig 14.5

tape loop

direction of spin

fig 14.6

fig 14.7

reels and handles

The choice whether to use a reel or handle is usually a very personal one, closely dictated by economics. Some fliers always use handles, whatever the type of line; others always reels; most use a mixture of both.

The handle or reel serves two purposes; it provides a convenient way of storing the line (which would otherwise become tangled), while more importantly, perhaps, also gives a comfortable means of holding on to and controlling the kite while in flight.

For lighter kites, simple, plastic handles can be purchased quite cheaply from most stores stocking kites. Depending on the size, this type is usually quite adequate for lines up to about 35 kg (75 lb) breaking strain.

SIMPLE HANDLES

The simplest form of handle is made from a short piece of dowel, anything from 12 mm (½ inch) diameter, to which the line is tied, then wound in a criss-cross fashion (Fig 15.1).

Cheap and simple.

CYLINDER REEL

This is a very simple reel. It is cheap, but can really only be used with very light line.

You will need a rigid circular container, wide cardboard tube or powdered milk container (with lid) or similar. Don't be tempted to use a tin or other metal, such as an aluminium drink can, which as well as cutting into your line can make nasty cuts in your fingers.

Take two lengths of dowel and tape them to opposite sides of the cylinder as shown. Fix hardboard or stiff cardboard circles to each end using a strong glue (Fig 15.2).

STUNTER GRIPS

Stunt fliers sometimes prefer soft grips rather than handles. These can be made from 2.5 cm (1 inch) wide nylon webbing and D-rings sewn as illustrated (Fig 15.3).

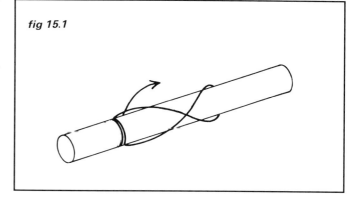

fig 15.1

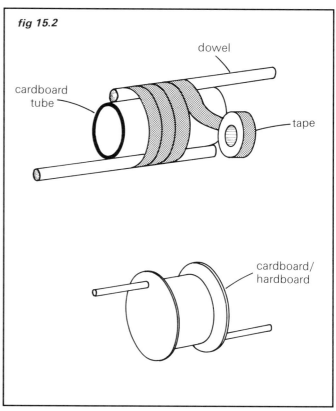

fig 15.2

dowel

cardboard tube

tape

cardboard/hardboard

LINE STORE

This is more a useful means of storing lines, particularly stunter line, although it can also be used as a handle (Fig 15.4). Dimensions can of course be altered to suit your own needs.

SMALL HANDLE

To make this and the larger handle you will need to learn some of the skills of using a coping saw or fretsaw.

Mark and cut out the shape in 5-ply wood to convenient dimensions (Fig 15.5), then carefully sand all edges.

Although it will be a little more expensive, try to buy waterproof plywood, sometimes called 'outdoor' plywood, which will be able to withstand rougher treatment and of course the occasional storm or dip in the sea.

LARGE HANDLE

This second handle has a slightly different shape and again dimensions can be chosen to suit the size of the line. Perhaps 30 cm (12 inches) by 15 cm (6 inches) might be average for a 50 kg (100 lb) line.

Mark out the shape on 7-ply wood, cut out and sand as above (Fig 15.6).

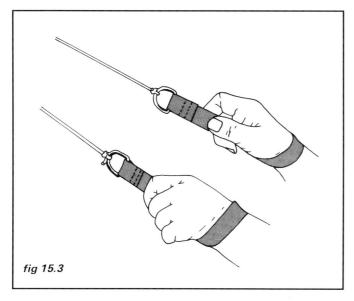

fig 15.3

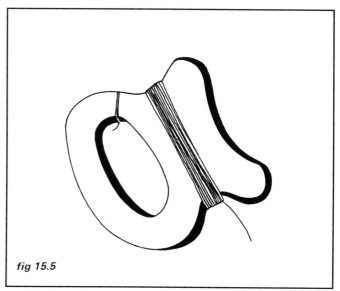

fig 15.5

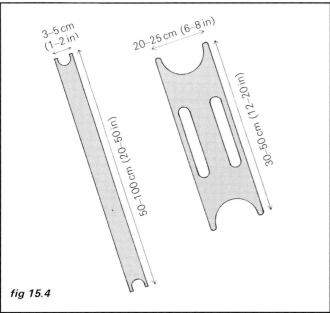

fig 15.4

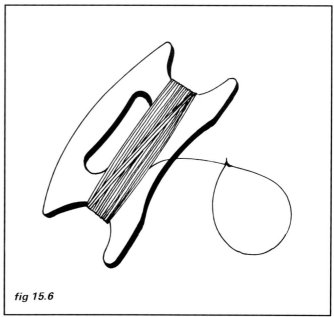

fig 15.6

further reading

BOOKS

Bushell, Helen, *Make Mine Fly* vols 1–3, 1985
Dunford, Don, *Kite Cookery*, 1979
Greger, Margaret, *Kites for Everyone*, 1984
Hart, Clive, *Kites: An Historical Survey*, 1967
Ito, Tishio & Komura, Hirorsuga, *Kites: The Science and Wonder*, 1979
Moulton, Ron, *Kites*, 1978
Pelham, David, *Penguin Book of Kites*, 1976
Picon, Daniel, *Cerf Volants*, 1985 (In French)
Eiji Ohashi, *Making Kite Trains*, 1978 (In Japanese – well illustrated)
Streeter, Tal, *Art of the Japanese Kite*, 1980
Takeshi Nishibayashi, *Create a Kite*, 1978 (In Japanese – well illustrated)

NEWSLETTERS AND MAGAZINES

British
Kiteflier. Quarterly. Started by Jon and Gill Bloom with John Barker in 1978, now Britain's most widely-circulated newsletter, and around which the Kite Society was formed. Packed with news of British and European events.
Kite. Quarterly. Newsletter of the Northern Kite Group. Of the British newsletters this is the longest surviving, well worth reading.
Aerodyne. Quarterly. Newsletter of the Brighton Kite Flyers, now distributed with *Kiteflier*. Mainly club notes but occasional good design/tips.
MKF Newsletter. Irregular. Newsletter of the Midlands Kite Fliers. As with *Aerodyne*, distributed with *Kiteflier*.
European Kiteflier. Only about half a dozen issues ever published in late 1970s but all packed with information. Worth borrowing copies.
Kites (Previously *Kitelines*). Newsletter of the British Kite Fliers Association. About six editions published in the late 1970s. Many of the designs later reprinted in Ron Moulton's book.

European
Vleiger. Quarterly. Journal of the Dutch Kite Society. Holland is without a doubt the European centre for kiteflying, reflected very much in this well produced and informative journal. Occasional articles in English.
Le Lucane. Irregular. Journal of the French Kite Society. If your French is up to it, well worth subscribing.
Le Journal de Nouveau Cervoloist Belge. Quarterly, Newsletter of the Belgian Kite Society. Although mostly in French, many articles are in English or with English summaries. Well worth subscribing, especially for its pirating of commercial designs!
Hoch Hinaus. Quarterly. Journal of the German Kite Society. Well written and illustrated but oh, so very serious.
Bulletino dell' Associazione Italiana Aquilonisti. Quarterly. Bulletin of the Italian Kite Association. Lots of club notes and announcements but occasionally you will find a gem with which to justify the subscription and all the struggle with the Italian.

North American
There are a large number of both United States and Canadian newsletters. *Kitelines* is the most widely distributed.
Kitelines. Quarterly. The world's leading kite magazine. Good colour photography, combined with expertly written articles.
Kite Tales. The predecessor to *Kitelines*, 1962–9. Provides an interesting insight into the development of the modern kite movement. Microfilm copies available from *Kitelines*.

kite suppliers – world listing

Kite Shops and Stores tend to come and go with the seasons and it is difficult to keep track. The following, however, are all well-established and can provide a range of kitemaking materials for the home constructor.

Belgium
DE WITTE UIL, Kammenstraat 14–16, B-2000 Antwerpen

Canada
CATCH THE WIND, 106 – 10th Street NW, Calgary, Alberta T2N 1V3
EARTH, WIND & SKY, 1501 – 8th Street East, Saskatoon, Saskachewan S7H 5J6
KITE DREAMS, 123 Carrie Cates Court, North Vancouver, B.C. V7M 3K7
ON THE WIND, 180 King Street West, Kitchener, Ontario N2G 4C5
TOUCH THE SKY, 836 Yonge Street, Toronto, Ontario M4W 2H1
VICTORIA KITE STORE, 102–560 Johnson Street, Victoria, B.C. V8W 3C6

Germany
DRACHENLADEN, 71 Münsterstrasse, D-4000 Düsseldorf 30
DRACHENSPEZIALIST, 103a Uerdingerstrasse, D-4005 Meerbusch 3
VOM WINDE VERWEHT, 81 Eisenacherstrasse, D-1000 Berlin 62
WOLKENSTÜRMER, 52 Hansastrasse, D-2000 Hamburg 13

Italy
VIVA DIDA, 31 via Ascanio Sforza, 2136 Milano

Netherlands
VLIEGER OP, 5-A Weteringkade, 2515-AK den Haag
VLIEGERWINKEL, 19 Nieuwe Hoogstraat, 1011-HD Amsterdam

Switzerland
DER SPIELER, 106 Hauptstrasse, CH-4102

United Kingdom
KITE STORE, 69 Neal Street, Covent Garden, London WC2H 9PJ
KITE & BALLOON CO, 128 Garratt Lane, Earlsfield, London SW18 4SU
GREENS OF BURNLEY, 226 Colne Road, Burnley, Lancs
MALVERN KITES, The Warehouse, St Anns Road, Great Malvern, Worcs

United States
California
ANTELOPE VALLEY KITEMAN, 2127 East Palmdale Boulevard, Palmdale, CA 93550
CATCH THE WIND, 1575 Spinnaker, 107-B Ventura, CA 93001
COLORS OF THE WIND, 2900 Main Street, Santa Monica, CA 90405
COME FLY A KITE, 1228 State Street, Santa Barbara, CA 93101
DAVE'S KITE CONNECTION, 15682 Sunflower, Huntington Beach, CA 92647
IN-FLIGHT KITES, 802 West 10th Street, Antioch, CA 94509
KITE CITY, 1201 Front Street, Old Sacramento, CA 95814
KITE COUNTRY, 566 Horton Plaza, San Diego, CA 92101
KITEMAKERS OF SAN FRANCISCO, 838 Grant, San Francisco, CA 94108
KITES & DELIGHTS, 2801 Leavenworth Street, San Francisco, CA 94133
LET'S FLY A KITE, 13755 Fiji Way, Marina del Rey, CA 90291
NORTH COAST KITES, 655 Shaw Avenue, Ferndale, CA 95536
SEAPORT KITE SHOP, 839-D West Harbor Drive, San Diego, CA 92101
THE KITE SHOP, 756 Plumas Street, Yuba City, CA 95991

WINDBORNE KITES, 585 Cannery Row, 105, M Monterey, CA 93940

Colorado
HI FLI KITES, London Square, 12101–C East Iliff, Aurora, CO 80014
INTO THE WIND, 2047 Broadway, Boulder, CO 80302
THE KITE STORE, Tabor Center, 1201 16th Street, Denver, CO 80202

Connecticut
ALL WIND SPORTS, 2434 Berlin Turnpike, Newington, CT 06111
MYSTIC KITE SHOP, 27-C Olde Mystick Village, Mystic, CT 06355

District of Columbia
THE KITE SITE, 3101 "M" Street N.W., Washington, DC 20007

Florida
ATLANTIC KITES, 3206 E. Atlantic Boulevard, Pompano Beach, FL 33062
CLOUD 9 KITES, 1122 E. Atlantic Avenue, Delray Beach, FL 33444
KITE WORLD, 109 South Miramar Avenue, Indialantic, FL 32903
KITERIGGERS, 3105 Spring Park Road, Jacksonville, FL 32207

Georgia
IDENTIFIED FLYING OBJECTS, 1164 Euclid Avenue NE, Atlanta, GA 30307
SAVANNAH SAILS & RAILS, 23 East River Street, Savannah, GA 31401

Hawaii
HIGH PERFORMANCE KITES, 1019 University Avenue, Honolulu, HI 96826
KITE FANTASY, 2863 Kalakaua Avenue, Honolulu, HI 96815

Illinois
AGAINST THE WIND, 3600 N. Main Street, Rockford, IL 61103

Indiana

KITECRAFT, 704 North College Avenue, Bloomington, IN 47401
THINGS THAT FLY, Union Station, 39 Jackson Street, Indianapolis, IN 46225

Louisianna

THE KITE LOFT, Riverwalk, 1 Podras, Space 90, New Orleans, LA 70130
THE KITE SHOP, Jackson Square, 542 St. Peter Street, New Orleans, LA 70116

Maryland

KITES AWEIGH, 6 Fleet Street, Annapolis, MD 21401
THE KITE LOFT, 511 Boardwalk, Ocean City, MD 21842
THE KITE LOFT, Harborplace, Light Street, Baltimore, MD 21202

Massachusetts

WORLD ON A STRING, 12 Bridge Street, Northampton, MA 01060

Michigan

FREE AIR KITE SHOP, 2830 E. Grand River, East Lansing, MI 48823
GRAND BAY KITE SHOP, 121 E. Front St., Traverse City, MI 49684
GRAND BAY KITE SHOP, 115 St. Joseph St., Suttons Bay, MI 49682
KITE KRAFT, 245 South Main, Frankenmuth, MI 48734
KITEMAN JACK'S, Newmand Street at the Pier, East Tawas, MI 48730
MACKINAW KITE COMPANY, 301 N. Harbor, Grand Haven, MI 49417
MACKINAW KITE COMPANY, 105 Huron St, Mackinaw City, MI 49701

Nevada

KITES 'N' MORE, 4601 W. Sahara Avenue, Las Vegas, NV 89102

New Jersey

HIGH FLY KITE COMPANY, 30 West End Avenue, Haddonfield, NJ 08033
SKY HIGH KITES, 50 Pitman Avenue, Ocean Grove, NJ 07756
WONDERFUL WORLD OF KITES, Peddler's Village, Booth 143, Route 35, Wall, NJ 08736

New York

CATCH A BREEZE, 26 Caroline Street, Saratoga Springs, NY 12866
GO FLY A KITE, 1201 Lexington Avenue, New York, NY 10028
WINDSOX, FLAGS & KITES, 976 Elmwood Avenue, Buffalo, NY 14222
WINDSOX, FLAGS & KITES, 2172 Niagara Falls Blvd, Tonawanda, NY 14150

North Carolina

KITES UNLIMITED, Atlantic Station Shopping Center, Atlantic Beach, NC 28512
KITES UNLIMITED, Crabtree Valley Mall, Raleigh, NC 27612
THE KITE KINGDOM, Sea Holly Square, MP 10, Kill Devil Hills, NC 27948

North Dakota

KITE HEIGHTS, 401 Broadway, Medora, ND 58645
PRAIRIE KITES, 120 North 3rd Street, Bismarck, ND 58501

Ohio

FLIGHTS OF FANCY, 22 South High Street, Dublin, OH 43017
THE KITE COMPANY, 4500 Chagrin River Road, Chagrin Falls, OH 44022

Oregon

CATCH THE WIND, 266 S. E. Highway 101, Lincoln City, OR 97367
CATCH THE WIND, 669 Bay, Newport, OR 97365
CATCH THE WIND, Agate Beach, Highway 101, Newport, OR 97365
CATCH THE WIND, 1250 Bay Street, Florence, OR 97439
FLYING THINGS, 1528 N. Highway 101, Lincoln City, OR 97367
ONCE UPON A BREEZE, 241 North Hemlock, Cannon Beach, OR 97110

Pennsylvania

A KITE AFFAIR, 900-A Eisenhower Blvd., Harrisburg, PA 17111
KLASSY KITES, King of Prussia Plaza, King of Prussia, PA 19406
THE MEADOW MOUSE, 520 N. Pennsylvania Ave, Morrisville, PA 19067

South Carolina

KLIG'S KITES, 9600 North Kings Highway, Myrtle Beach, SC 29577
KLIG'S KITES, Myrtle Beach Pavilion, Myrtle Beach, SC 29577
KLIG'S KITES, Deerfield Plaza, Highway 17, Surfside Beach, SC 29577
KLIG'S KITES, Main Ocean Drive Section, North Myrtle Beach, SC 29582

Texas

KITES ETC., 202 Valley View Center, Dallas, TX 75202
WIND WALKER KITE SHOP, 120 S. Highway 208, Clute, TX 77531

Utah

KITES AND THINGS, 460 Trolley Square, Salt Lake City, UT 84102
NATURE'S WAY KITE SHOP, 416 E. 900 S., Salt Lake City, UT 84111

Virginia

KRAZY KITES, 1353 Mill Dam Road, Virginia Beach, VA 23454
THE KITE BOX, 1552 East Main Street, Richmond, VA 23219
THE KITE KINGDOM, 333 Waterside Drive, Norfolk, VA 23510
THE KITE KOOP, Landmark Plaza, North Main Street, Chincotegue, VA 23336

Washington

CITY KITES, 1501 Western Avenue, Seattle, WA 98101
GREAT WINDS, 402 Occidental Avenue South, Seattle, WA 98104
LONG BEACH KITES, 104 Pacific Avenue N., Long Beach, WA 98631
SUSPENDED ELEVATIONS, 1915 North 34th Street, Seattle, WA 98103

Wisconsin

FISH CREEK KITE COMPANY, 3853 Highway 42, Fish Creek, WI 54212
FOUR WINDS KITE CO., N70 W6340 Bridge Road, Cedarburg, WI 53102

The above listing is reproduced courtesy of Valerie Govig and *Kitelines*.

index